Ancient Mesopotamia

An Enthralling Overview of Mesopotamian History, Starting from Eridu through the Sumerians, Akkadians, Assyrians, Hittites, and Persians to Alexander the Great

© Copyright 2022

All Rights Reserved. No part of this book may be reproduced in any form without permission in writing from the author. Reviewers may quote brief passages in reviews.

Disclaimer: No part of this publication may be reproduced or transmitted in any form or by any means, mechanical or electronic, including photocopying or recording, or by any information storage and retrieval system, or transmitted by email without permission in writing from the publisher.

While all attempts have been made to verify the information provided in this publication, neither the author nor the publisher assumes any responsibility for errors, omissions or contrary interpretations of the subject matter herein.

This book is for entertainment purposes only. The views expressed are those of the author alone, and should not be taken as expert instruction or commands. The reader is responsible for his or her own actions.

Adherence to all applicable laws and regulations, including international, federal, state and local laws governing professional licensing, business practices, advertising and all other aspects of doing business in the US, Canada, UK or any other jurisdiction is the sole responsibility of the purchaser or reader.

Neither the author nor the publisher assumes any responsibility or liability whatsoever on the behalf of the purchaser or reader of these materials. Any perceived slight of any individual or organization is purely unintentional.

Free limited time bonus

Stop for a moment. We have a free bonus set up for you. The problem is this: we forget 90% of everything that we read after 7 days. Crazy fact, right? Here's the solution: we've created a printable, 1-page pdf summary for this book that you're reading now. All you have to do to get your free pdf summary is to go to the following website: **https://livetolearn.lpages.co/enthrallinghistory/**

Once you do, it will be intuitive. Enjoy, and thank you!

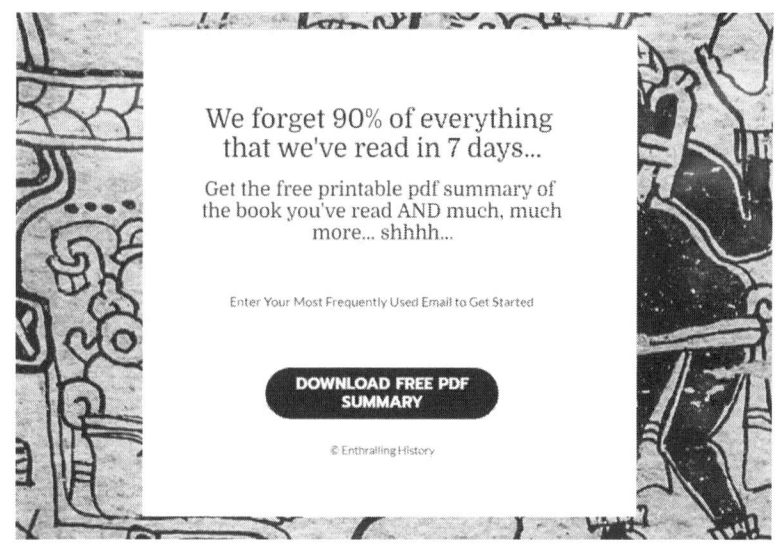

Contents

INTRODUCTION 1
PART ONE: AN AGE OF FIRSTS (5500-2000 BCE) 5
CHAPTER 1 - ERIDU: THE FIRST CITY 6
CHAPTER 2 - SUMERIANS: THE FIRST CIVILIZATION 17
CHAPTER 3 - SARGON OF AKKAD: THE FIRST RULER.................... 30
CHAPTER 4 - AKKAD: THE FIRST EMPIRE 42
PART TWO: AGE OF EMPIRES (2000-539 BCE) 54
CHAPTER 5 - ASSYRIA: AN OVERVIEW 55
CHAPTER 6 - DAILY LIFE IN ASSYRIA 68
CHAPTER 7 - BABYLON: AN OVERVIEW 80
CHAPTER 8 - BABYLON: RELIGION, MYTH, AND CREATION 93
PART THREE: AGE OF INNOVATION 105
CHAPTER 9 - THE EPIC OF GILGAMESH... 106
CHAPTER 10 - INNOVATIONS AND INVENTIONS 117
CHAPTER 11 - KING HAMMURABI AND HIS CODE......................... 128
CHAPTER 12 - ZOROASTRIANISM 140
PART FOUR: HERE COME THE PERSIANS (550 BCE-330 BCE) 153
CHAPTER 13 - THE ACHAEMENID EMPIRE RISES 154
CHAPTER 14 - EVERYDAY LIFE IN PERSIA.. 166
CHAPTER 15 - PERSIAN ART, ARCHITECTURE, AND
TECHNOLOGY 178

CHAPTER 16 – PERSIA'S GREAT ENEMY: ALEXANDER THE GREAT 193
CONCLUSION 207
HERE'S ANOTHER BOOK BY ENTHRALLING HISTORY THAT YOU MIGHT LIKE 212
FREE LIMITED TIME BONUS 213
BIBLIOGRAPHY 214

Introduction

"All the evil winds, all stormy winds gathered into one and with them, the Flood was sweeping over the land, for seven days and seven nights. After the Flood had swept over the country, after the evil wind had tossed the big boat about on the great waters, the sun came out spreading light over heaven and earth."

The Eridu Genesis from a Sumerian cuneiform tablet, circa 1600 BCE

Sound familiar? The *Eridu Genesis* flood story echoes other ancient Mesopotamian flood stories, such as those found in the Hebrew Torah, the Sumerian *Epic of Gilgamesh*, and the Akkadian *Epic of Atrahasis*. Mesopotamia, "the cradle of civilization," gave birth to the world's first pieces of literature and many other innovations, including the first agricultural systems, the first cities, the first writing system, the first wheel, the first maps, the first sailboats, the first written mathematics, the first kings, and the first great empires. Mesopotamia was indeed a land of many beginnings!

This overview gives an in-depth insight into the intriguing people of ancient Mesopotamia and their astonishing achievements. Traveling back 7,400 years, we will begin with ancient Eridu, the first city of southern Mesopotamia. We will then explore the Sumerian civilization, the Akkadian Empire, the Assyrians, the Hittites, the Persian-Achaemenid Empire, and end with Alexander the Great of Macedonia, who conquered most of Mesopotamia. We will unlock the mysteries of these ancient people, explain the distinctive features of the various civilizations, and discover what made them exceptional.

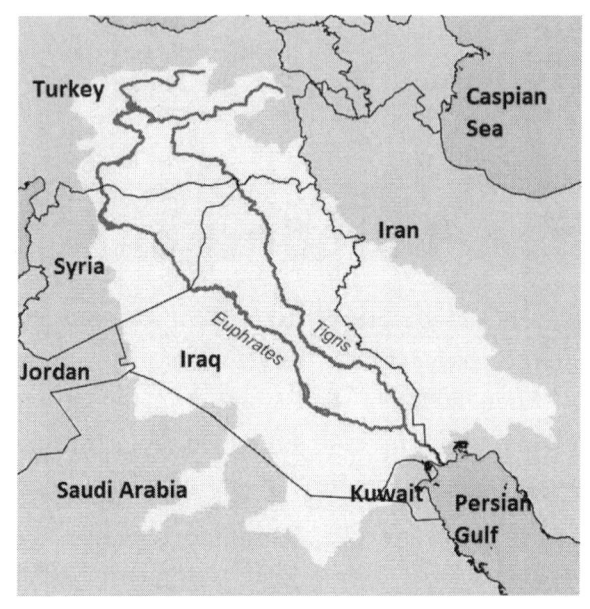

The great Euphrates and Tigris Rivers flow through Mesopotamia.

Credit: No machine-readable author provided. Kmusser assumed (based on copyright claims)., CC BY-SA 2.5 https://creativecommons.org/licenses/by-sa/2.5 via Wikimedia Commons;https://commons.wikimedia.org/wiki/File:Tigr-euph.png)

Where is Mesopotamia? It encompasses part of the Middle East. Mesopotamia literally means "between the rivers," referring to the Euphrates and Tigris, which the Torah said flowed out of the Garden of Eden. Both rivers flow from Turkey's Taurus Mountains through Syria, meeting in Iraq, then flowing together through Iran and into the Persian Gulf. Ancient Mesopotamia included modern-day Iraq and Kuwait, as well as portions of Iran, Turkey, Syria, and Saudi Arabia.

Many books written about ancient Mesopotamia were written by scholars for other scholars, which means they use academic language. Some were written decades before the most recent archaeological finds and the latest information. Other books are meant for children or cover specific aspects of Mesopotamian civilization. This comprehensive overview draws from scholarly research yet endeavors to unlock Mesopotamia's majestic history in clear, compelling, easy-to-understand prose. It is great for beginners and history buffs alike.

Knowledge of past civilizations helps us discern our world today. We will discover how Mesopotamia's ancient civilizations contributed to today's cultures. How did they inform our worldview and lay the foundation for our belief systems? How do the catalysts for change in ancient Mesopotamia, the rise and fall of great empires, impact us today? How have the struggles of ancient Mesopotamia influenced contemporary Middle Eastern conflicts?

This overview is divided into four sections, beginning with "An Age of Firsts," when people began forming agricultural communities, domesticating animals, and devising irrigation techniques that took advantage of the Tigris and Euphrates Rivers. We will explore Eridu, the first of five cities established before the Great Flood, according to the *Sumerian King List*.

We will then examine the Sumerians, who developed the earliest written language and built Ur, the patriarch Abraham's birthplace. This city was seven miles northeast of Eridu and fifty miles southeast of Uruk, the hero Gilgamesh's city. What spurred their sophisticated architecture, notably the terraced pyramid-shaped ziggurat towers? How did trade expand their territory? We will analyze the Code of Ur-Nammu, the world's oldest law code. What did it say about witchcraft, runaway slaves, and bodily injury? We will also look at Sargon the Great, who conquered all of Macedonia and part of Syria, Lebanon, Turkey, and Iran, establishing the Akkadian, the first empire in recorded history.

Part Two, "Age of Empires," delves into Assyria and Babylonia, the mighty empires that ruled Mesopotamia. How did they take control, what made them famous, and who were some of their renowned leaders? What intriguing aspects of ordinary people's lives can we learn from archaeology and ancient documents? How did the Amorites seize control and establish Babylon as their capital? What was the Babylonians' religion, and what was their creation myth? And what led to the collapse of the Assyrian and Babylonian Empires?

Part Three, "Age of Innovation," dives into the adventures of King Gilgamesh and his half-wild companion Enkidu in the *Epic of Gilgamesh*. We will discover the incredible innovations and inventions that took place from 1800 to 1400 BCE. How did the famous King Hammurabi expand his empire, and what laws did he include in his law code? What happened when the Elamites conquered Ur?

When Nebuchadnezzar conquered Mesopotamia, including Jerusalem in 586 BCE, why did he take the Jews into captivity? What happened to them in Babylon? Did Babylon really have hanging gardens? What inspired the ornate Ishtar Gate and the walls of Babylon? How did the Zoroastrian religion influence Mesopotamian culture and other beliefs?

Part Four, "Here Come the Persians," uncovers how Cyrus the Great seized power and founded the Achaemenid Empire. We will explore everyday life in Persia and review the exquisite Persian art, stunning architecture, and extraordinary technology that changed the known world. How did the clash play out between King Darius III and Persia's great enemy, Alexander the Great?

Now, let's step back seventy-four centuries to begin our exploration of Mesopotamia. Why was Mesopotamia's legacy so revolutionary? And how has it molded society as we know it today?

PART ONE: An Age of Firsts (5500–2000 BCE)

Chapter 1 – Eridu: The First City

If you visited the site of the world's oldest city today, you would see an unprepossessing mound rising over a vast expanse of desolate desert. If you looked closer, you'd realize what looks like a natural mesa is actually the crumbling ruins of ancient buildings. The mound is a tell, the accumulated stratified debris of a city occupied from around 5400 BCE until the 5th century BCE. Houses, temples, and cemeteries were built on top of old ones for millennia, creating an artificial hill.

Eridu wasn't always located in a barren wasteland. If you traveled back in time thousands of years, you'd find a prosperous, bustling metropolis covering one hundred acres on the northern shores of the Persian Gulf, close to the mouth of the Euphrates River. Outside the city walls, the fertile wetlands of Lake Hammar, which was fed by the Euphrates, came right up to the city's eastern wall. The lake is saline today, but it was freshwater in ancient times, according to an archaeological and geological survey from 2010. A canal came in from the lake and around the northern and western walls of the city, with channels irrigating the agricultural fields and fruit groves. Farther away were the vast pasturelands, where sheep and goats grazed. In the wetlands, workers would press clay and mud into forms that would dry in the sun, forming bricks.

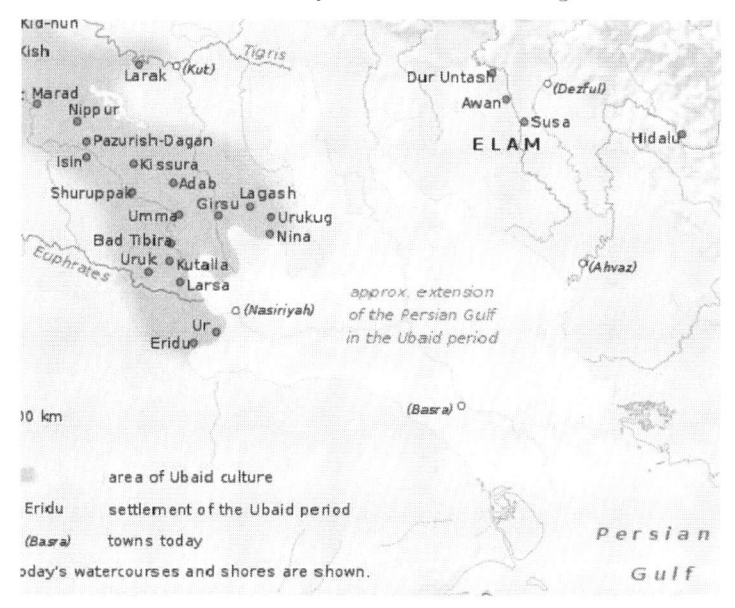

Thousands of years ago, the Persian Gulf extended far north to Eridu and Ur.

Credit: NordNordWest, usingUbaid culture sites map.jpg by John D. CroftGroßer Atlas zur Weltgeschichte, Westermann SchulbuchverlagPutzger Historischer Weltaltas, Cornelsen Verlagdtv-Atlas Weltgeschichte, Deutscher Taschenbuch VerlagGTOPO-30 Elevation Data by USGS, CC BY-SA 3.0 https://creativecommons.org/licenses/by-sa/3.0 via Wikimedia Commons; https://commons.wikimedia.org/wiki/File:Map_Ubaid_culture-en.svg

Moving south, you would find fishermen in picturesque sailboats on the Persian Gulf, casting their nets. Along its shore, people would be harvesting shellfish and drying fish on platforms. Other boats would trade up the Euphrates or with other settlements around the Gulf. You would hear the grunts and grumbles of camels as they set out in caravans, following the Fertile Crescent north into what is now Turkey, east to the Mediterranean, and down its shores past Sidon and Tyre to Egypt.

Enki's temple, the House of the Aquifer, stood in the city center inside the city walls. The original temple dates to 5300 BCE, when Ur was a settlement of the Ubaid civilization. The first temple was a modest one-room structure with an altar for sacrifices at one end and a cult niche for an idol at the other. Grander temples were built over the first site as time passed; there were eighteen of them over several thousand years. In the 3rd millennium BCE, a multi-storied, tiered pyramid-shaped temple called a ziggurat towered over the city rooflines. Adobe brick residential buildings that housed four thousand people surrounded the thirty-acre city center.

The Ziggurat of Enki may have looked like this model.
https://commons.wikimedia.org/wiki/File:SumerianZiggurat.jpg

Do we know for sure if Eridu was the world's oldest city? The *Sumerian King List* identified Eridu as the first city (of five), as does Babylonian literature. Archaeological excavations at Eridu revealed constructions from the prehistoric Ubaid period (6500–3800 BCE), with the first structures dating to about 5400 BCE. Urbanization first began in Mesopotamia before China, India, or Egypt. So, which Mesopotamian city, if not Eridu, came first?

Scholars sometimes propose Uruk was the oldest city, but archaeological evidence suggests it was first settled around 5000 BCE, about four centuries after Eridu. The ancient city of Jericho is another contender, and it does have evidence of human occupation going back to the Neolithic Age. However, it did not reach city status (in terms of population size) until the Bronze Age, which was after Eridu. A third contender is Çatalhöyük in Turkey, which did have a settlement of several thousand people prior to Eridu. However, it lacked a city's infrastructure; it didn't even have streets! People had to get around on the rooftops.

Depending on one's definition of what a city actually *is* (and archaeologists and other scholars hotly debate this), Eridu takes the prize as the oldest settlement that: 1) was the center of religion for the surrounding area, 2) was densely populated, 3) had a central government, and 4) had infrastructure. As Enki's main sanctuary, Eridu was a religious center of Mesopotamia until the 6th century BCE. According to Sumerian mythology, Enki, the god of deep waters, magic, and wisdom, was Eridu's founder.

Eridu started as a cluster of people living in reed-thatched huts. They had herds of goats and sheep, fished from the Persian Gulf and the nearby Lake Hammar, and hunted waterfowl, gazelle, deer, and other wild animals. They engaged in simple agriculture and began growing grain. Einkorn wheat grew wild throughout the region, and they learned to cultivate it. The early settlers had an adequate and healthy diet with plenty of protein, mainly fish, and their population quickly grew. Over time, sun-dried clay-brick houses replaced the reed structures. Eventually, they began building multi-storied buildings, and their humble beginnings grew into a stunning city!

This pottery jar dates to the Ubaid III period (5300-4700 BCE).
Credit: ALFGRN CC BY-SA 2.0 https://creativecommons.org/licenses/by-sa/2.0, via Wikimedia Commons; https://commons.wikimedia.org/w/index.php?curid=78172134

They began producing a type of pottery called Hadji Muhammed ceramics with striking geometric patterns. They built canal networks to irrigate their fields. They also started trading with what is now Turkey for obsidian, black volcanic glass or igneous rock from which they formed knife blades and weapons.

At the end of the Ubaid period (around 3800 BCE), Eridu lost most of its population. Nearby Ur, which was just several miles away along the coast, was also simultaneously uninhabited for a time. A layer of sediment in Ur indicates a flood swept over it, covering the city in silt. A flood of this magnitude may have impacted its neighbor Eridu, although Ur was much closer to the cojoined Euphrates-Tigris River system.

Lake Hammar's levels fell due to over-irrigation and climate change, making its water more saline and harmful to the crops. The land became arider since there was less rainfall, turning it from semi-desert to desert. As the lake levels dropped, sand dunes formed around the lake's perimeter that may have cut off the irrigation canals. For centuries, Eridu and its neighbors lay abandoned under the desert sun.

Around 2900 BCE, Eridu was again inhabited, and it grew into a major city. By this time, Semitic-speaking herdsmen were entering the area. An unknown king, or more likely a series of kings over time, built a grand palace with dozens of rooms, buttresses, and drains for water. Eridu went into decline again by 2050 BCE, and it was uninhabited or sparsely inhabited after this point. In the 7th century BCE, the Neo-Babylonians rebuilt its temple site, honoring Enki's city. However, it never rose as a city again. The receding Persian Gulf eventually left almost two hundred miles of desert between the city and the sea, which had once been its source of food and trade. The rising salinity of the available water supply could not provide enough fresh water to sustain life and support agriculture.

Although Eridu was located almost within sight of Ur and other cities that shared a common language, religion, and culture, each was an independent political entity with its own king: a city-state. Eridu and its neighboring city-states consisted of a densely-populated urban residential area with narrow streets that wandered through the maze of buildings. In the city's center stood a temple, palace, markets, and public buildings

Tall, thick walls encircled Eridu to protect it from neighboring city-states. Outside the walls stretched lush, irrigated farms; sheep, goats, and camels grazed along the wetlands. Like other city-states of southern Mesopotamia, Eridu was a politically self-contained bubble, with enough agriculture, domesticated animals, and fish to sustain its population. However, trade was an essential element of Mesopotamian culture, especially long-distance transactions in lands with resources like metal ore, which the people used to make weapons and farming utensils. Camel caravans traveled overland, and boats on the Euphrates and the Persian Gulf were trade conduits.

Eridu had three different ecosystems. The first was agricultural, with an extensive canal and irrigation system necessary in a semi-desert climate with limited rainfall. Like most early Mesopotamian regions, the people grew barley and einkorn wheat. Under the shade of date palms, farmers grew beans, cucumbers, garlic, leeks, lettuce, and peas. They also grew fruit, including pomegranates, grapes, figs, and melons.

Archaeological digs in Eridu unearthed models of sailboats used on the Persian Gulf.
https://commons.wikimedia.org/wiki/File:pERSIAN.jpg

The second ecosystem was mainly sea-based. Eridu was a coastal city in ancient times, and fish was the primary protein source. Archaeological excavations have discovered whole rooms full of dried fish! Extensive middens (refuse heaps) along the Persian Gulf reveal that shellfish harvesting was vital for food and exquisite pearls. Shells would be pressed into the walls of palaces, temples, and homes, acting as decorations.

In the area around Eridu, nomadic herders of camels, goats, and sheep lived in tents, tending about 1,400 sheep in flocks of about 70 animals (the ancient cuneiform tablets recorded information on the herds). The nomads milked the ewes to make butter, yogurt, and cheese. They used their wool for clothing and slaughtered the animals for sacrifices and meat. In addition to domestic animals, gazelle and wild ass herds roamed the grasslands of the river and lake system, which were hunted for meat and skins.

In Eridu and other early Mesopotamian cities, the kings were first known as *Ensi* or priest-kings. Later, as cities grew and needed more complex leadership, the king became primarily a secular ruler called *Lugal* or strongman. The strongman-king of Eridu administered the work of farmers, fishermen, and herdsmen, and he oversaw the merchants, craftsmen, and construction workers within the city.

Although the king continued having a dual role of city-administrator and religious leader, a priestly caste evolved to perform sacrifices and other religious rites and to gaze at the stars to discover omens. The people believed the heavens chose the king; to obey their king was to obey the gods. The king was considered the intermediary between the people and the gods. In addition to administrative and religious functions, the strongman-king protected Eridu from invasion, led his men in wars against other city-states, supported law and order in the city, and provided for widows and orphans.

The farmers, herders, fishermen, and workers, who built and maintained the dams and irrigation canals, mostly lived in villages or nomadic tent dwellings around the city. The craftspeople—carpenters, weavers, and blacksmiths—lived within the city, along with the priests and administrators.

In the earliest days of Eridu, people discovered that intense heat could shape metal. They also found that heating rocks like azurite and malachite released copper. As their knowledge of metallurgy evolved, they learned they could mix copper with tin to produce stronger bronze. By 4000 BCE, the people of Eridu and other Mesopotamian cities were using bronze, copper, gold, iron, lead, mercury, silver, and tin.

A city the size of Eridu required a bureaucracy of city officials, tax collectors, and scribes to keep records. The farmers, herders, craftsmen, and other workers paid a tithe or part of their product to the city to pay for the cost of the defensive wall around the city, the irrigation canals and aqueducts, and other infrastructure. By 3500 BCE, a pictograph writing system had developed in Mesopotamia, and clerks used cuneiform writing to track taxes, merchants' and traders' sales, and other vital information.

Writing in Eridu began with pictographs like these.
https://en.wikipedia.org/wiki/Cuneiform#/media/File:Tableta_con_trillo.png

By 3200 BCE, Eridu's scribes were using cuneiform writing, making wedge-shaped indentations with a reed stylus onto clay tablets. They also began chiseling cuneiform into stone. The cuneiform marks represented syllables, and putting them together formed words. As writing developed, the first schools opened to teach some young people how to read and write. Early writing was mainly used for administrative purposes, but scholars also put oral traditions and histories into written form.

The *Eridu Genesis* (the *Sumerian Flood Story*), an ancient Sumerian text written approximately 2300 BCE, might be the oldest Mesopotamian account of the Great Flood. A similar story later appeared in the *Epic of Gilgamesh* (circa 2150 BCE), the *Epic of Atrahasis* (circa 1640 BCE), and a detailed description in the Hebrew Bereshit (Genesis, circa 1446 BCE). These accounts likely retold stories from older documents or oral tradition.

Fragments of the *Eridu Genesis* are found on several clay tablets; the first one was discovered in ancient Nippur, Iraq. The tablets have been broken or damaged and have missing lines; however, what is there is clearly an account of a Great Flood story. Scholars relied on the later *Epic of Atrahasis* to fill in the missing sentences. In the *Eridu Genesis*, the righteous man chosen to survive the deluge and continue human life is Ziusudra, the priest-king of Suruppak. In the *Epic of Gilgamesh*, he is called Utnapishtim. In the *Epic of Atrahasis*, he is Atrahasis, and in Genesis, he is Noah.

The *Eridu Genesis* begins with the mother-goddess Nintur leading humans back from their trails and having them build brick cities with temples. There, she can relax in the cool shade, and the people could live in peace, practicing divination. Then she instituted the kingship, saying the king was to advise the people, oversee their labor, and teach them to follow like cattle. A royal scepter, a crown, and a regal throne descended from heaven.

The people built the first city, Eridu, and the goddess appointed Nudimmud as its king. Four other cities were built with four other kings. The people dredged irrigation canals, which enabled abundant crops. But they made so much noise while they worked that they annoyed Enlil, the god of the wind, earth, and storms. Enlil colluded with the other gods to kill mankind.

Distraught, the mother-goddess Nintur wept over her creatures, and the god Enki, who had founded the city of Eridu, determined to save humankind. He warned the priest-king Ziusudra. "Listen! Heed my advice! A flood will sweep over the cities and the country. The gods decided to destroy mankind! Their command is irrevocable!"

Enki counseled Ziusudra to build a great ark and load it with pairs of animals. Then the winds blew, and the flood swept over the cities for seven days and nights as the ark tossed about on the raging sea. Finally, the sun came out, spreading light through the sky and down onto the earth. Ziusudra cut an opening in the boat, and the sun shone inside. Ziusudra stepped out in front of the sun, kissing the ground.

Ziusudra then butchered oxen and many sheep to sacrifice, along with barley cakes. At this point, the enraged Enlil discovered Ziusudra had survived the flood. Enki explained his actions, saying the man was an ally with the gods. Ziusudra then kissed the ground and honored Enlil and his father, the supreme god An (or Anu), and the gods rewarded Ziusudra with immortality. Ziusudra guided the animals off the ark and went to live in the east, over the mountains of Dilmun.

Another Mesopotamian myth tells of Inanna, the patron goddess of Uruk and the daughter of Enki, the patron god of Eridu. According to the myth, Inanna traveled fifty miles south from Uruk to Eridu to persuade her father to give her the *mes* (gifts of civilization) for her fledgling city. At first, Enki refused. So, Inanna challenged him to a drinking contest. When he was drunk, he gave the *mes* to Inanna. The following day, he awoke with a dreadful hangover. He realized what he'd done and tried to retrieve the *mes* from Inanna. But she had already fled the scene and was back in Uruk, developing it into a great city.

This myth seems to represent the transition in power from Eridu to Uruk. The southern cities became less important (or faded away altogether) while Uruk became the new power center. The Torah records that the patriarch Terah (Abraham's father) packed up his extended family and left Ur (seven miles from Eridu), following the Euphrates north with his sheep, goats, and camels to Haran. According to genealogies, this emigration was around 2100 BCE. Perhaps it was part of an extensive migration north from the Eridu-Ur region.

Chapter 2 – Sumerians: The First Civilization

For over two thousand years, the scorching sands of Iraq and Kuwait hid the relics of the Sumerians: the world's first civilized group of people. Sumer, the "cradle of civilization," lay in southern Mesopotamia, stretching along the Euphrates and Tigris Rivers to the Persian Gulf. *Sumer*, an Akkadian word, means "land of the civilized kings." The Hebrews called the land *Shinar*, "land of two rivers." But the Sumerians' name for their land was *kiengir*, simply meaning "the land," and they called themselves *sagiga*, the "black-headed people."

Three of their earliest cities were Eridu, Uruk, and Ur, which were all settled during the prehistoric Ubaid period (c. 6500-3800 BC). However, Eridu and Ur were abandoned and then reinhabited by the Sumerians at the cusp of the Bronze Age (3500 BCE). By that time, the Sumerian language, which is unrelated to any known language group, was the dominant language of southern Mesopotamia.

The Sumerians built most of their cities on the Tigris and Euphrates Rivers or their tributaries. City-states were usually independent entities, but occasionally, a strong leader of one city-state would conquer and absorb other city-states into his kingdom. King Eannatum of Lagash is a prime example. He drove out Elamite invaders and then conquered Ur, Uruk, Kish, and other Sumerian cities, forming a small empire.

The *Sumerian King List* provides invaluable information on the kings of each era and the eras' most important cities. The earliest kings, before the Great Flood, lived fantastically long lives: eight kings ruled for a total of 385,200 years. After the flood, the kings enumerated in the *Sumerian King List* gradually had shorter lives, similar to the genealogies in the Torah, where lifespans grew much shorter after the Great Flood.

After Gilgamesh's rule, most kings reigned for less than a century and often less than a decade. The latter part of the *Sumerian King List* following Gilgamesh is probably actual history and not mythical. Excavations from Sumer back up part of the *Sumerian King List*, such as grave markers and other artifacts that recorded the names of the kings.

Archaeology also confirms that before 5000 BCE, the Sumerians had already established an agrarian society. The people worked with stone tools, including adzes (a digging tool similar to an ax), hoes, knives, and sickles. By this time, they were also making bricks for construction, creating striking painted pottery, and sculpting intriguing figurines, some with sci-fi appearances, such as reptilian people or individuals with elongated necks or enormous round eyes.

The Sumerians' well-rounded diet featured fish, cheese, and yogurt for their main protein, and it was occasionally supplemented with mutton or wild game. They ate bread and porridge made from einkorn wheat, millet, or barley and consumed various fruit and vegetables, including pomegranates, dates, lentils, chickpeas, melons, and cucumbers.

A husband-and-wife toast each other while drinking beer (this time without a straw).

Credit: Osama Shukir Muhammed Amin FRCP(Glasg), CC BY-SA 4.0
https://creativecommons.org/licenses/by-sa/4.0 via Wikimedia Commons;
https://commons.wikimedia.org/wiki/File:Detail._Part_of_the_so-called_Banquet_Plaques._Beer_was_a_common_daily_dietary_staple_in_ancient_Mesopotamia._From_Ur,_Iraq._Early_Dynastic_Period,_2900-2350_BCE._Sulaymaniyah_Museum,_Iraqi_Kurdistan.jpg

They needed to drink lots of water in the hot, dry climate, which they kept in earthenware pots. Water would condense on the surface of these large jars, keeping the water cool. The people also drank beer! They even had a goddess of beer: Ninkasi. The world's first recipe for brewing beer comes from the Sumerians in the *Hymn to Ninkasi*. Beer was a bit different then. It had about the same alcohol content as today, but it had a thick, milkshake consistency. Like we drink milkshakes with straws, the Sumerians often drank their beer through long straws from large jugs; several people would drink from the same jar. A recurring theme in Sumerian pottery art was a husband making love to his wife while she drank beer from a straw!

Homes were initially made from bundled marsh reeds and later replaced by mud-brick houses with arched doorways and flat roofs. Families enjoyed gathering on the rooftops in the cool evenings and usually slept there. They would also spread grain or grapes out to dry on their roofs. Temples, palaces, and other grander-scale buildings featured elaborate constructions with terracotta decorations, bronze accents, mosaics, columns, and mural paintings. Relief carvings in stone, which had remarkably realistic figures, adorned many Sumerian temples. Sumerians surged ahead in metal-casting technology, which they used for some sculptures.

Sumerian men and women wore wraparound wool or sheepskin skirts that fell to their knees or ankles—longer skirts showed higher status. Men usually wore no clothing above the waist in the heat of the day. The women's skirts often had a section wrapped over one shoulder, sometimes leaving one breast exposed. Both men and women wore earrings, necklaces, and bracelets of gold, turquoise, and lapis lazuli.

The highly innovative Sumerian people engaged in complex and cooperative efforts, such as building thick, high city walls, complex irrigation systems, magnificent ziggurats, and splendid palaces. After inventing the world's first writing system—pictographs that evolved into cuneiform—they wrote down the world's first literature: epic poetry, hymns, and prayers. They also used their writing system for law codes and administrative record-keeping.

Sumerians used herbalism and magic in their medical practices but learned to extract chemicals from plants and other substances to produce medications. They had an advanced understanding of anatomy, and doctors performed surgeries (archaeologists have unearthed surgical instruments). They understood that bodily organs could malfunction, causing illness. Cuneiform tablets dating to 1770 BCE demonstrate knowledge of lethal pathogens.

The Sumerians made astounding advances in hydraulic engineering. Not only did they invent crop irrigation, harnessing the Euphrates and Tigris for their agricultural fields, but they also learned to build ditches and dikes to control the frequent flooding of these great rivers. Their skill in these engineering feats, not to mention their stunning architecture, demonstrates their sophisticated knowledge of measurements, geometry, calculus, and trigonometry.

Sumerians believed in an assortment of gods with human-like forms: anthropomorphic polytheism. Each city-state had a patron deity and was the terrestrial home of that god. In their core pantheon, An (Anu) ruled as the supreme god of heaven. Enki (Ea) was the god of the earth, healing, and groundwater. He was Eridu's patron god and protected humans when the other gods wanted to kill them. Enlil (Nunamnir) was the god of the atmosphere and wind. An, Enlil, and Enki formed a triad that ruled heaven, earth, and the underworld.

Inanna, the patron deity of Uruk, was the planet Venus's divine personification; she represented love, sex, beauty, justice, political power, and war. The Akkadians, Assyrians, and Babylonians worshiped her as Ishtar. Inanna's twin brother, Utu, was the sun god and represented truth and morality. Sin (or Nanna) was Enlil's son; he was the moon god and represented wisdom.

The Sumerians thought that mankind's reason for existing was to serve the gods. If they failed to please the gods, humans would suffer. If a flood destroyed a village, it was because the people had offended the gods. Thus, they needed priests to engage in rituals to discern the gods' will and what people needed to do to stay on their good side. The Sumerian priests were astrologers. They read omens and predicted the future from the stars, planets, and sun. All Sumerians were expected to pray daily to the gods, honoring them with hymns and incense, and atone for their sins. They prayed while raising both hands in the air or with one hand in front of their mouths. They often kneeled or prostrated themselves face-down on the ground.

This silver lion's head guarded the entrance of Puabi's burial chamber.

Credit: Mary Harrsch, CC BY 2.0 https://creativecommons.org/licenses/by/2.0 via Wikimedia Commons; https://commons.wikimedia.org/wiki/File:Silver_Lion%27s_Head_Finial_for_the_arm_of_a_chair_with_shell_and_lapis_lazuli_inset_eyes_recovered_from_the_royal_cemetery_of_Ur_2550-2450_BCE.jpg

One astonishing ritual was how the Sumerians buried their dead, particularly their royalty. British archaeologist Leonard Woolley discovered Ur's "death pit" in 1926, where the priestess-queen Puabi was buried around 2600 BCE. More than one hundred attendants and soldiers, draped with gold and silver, were sacrificed to accompany her to the afterlife. Woolley unearthed a staggering amount of treasure in her tomb: a spectacular golden headdress with gold leaves, a lyre with a gold and lapis-lazuli bull's head, gold tableware, gold and lapis lazuli necklaces and belts, and a chariot covered with silver.

Ur's location on the Persian Gulf at the mouth of the Euphrates-Tigris made it an important trade city with astounding wealth. Surrounded by marshy land, farming was relatively easy. In fact, sophisticated farming techniques may not have been necessary to support a relatively large population since abundant fish, waterfowl, tubers, and other food sources were readily available. Ur was, however, susceptible to frequent flooding.

A small settlement existed there from about 5000 BCE until 3800 BCE. At that time, Ur experienced a devastating flood, leaving an eleven-foot layer of silt that was discovered by archaeologists. By 3500 BCE, it was inhabited again, and it eventually grew into a city of thirty-four thousand people. The extravagance and wealth with which the priestess-queen Puabi was buried imply an advanced and wealthy civilization.

King Mesannepadda initiated the First Dynasty of Ur (2500-2445 BCE), gaining ascendency over the city of Uruk, which had been dominating Sumer. Four kings followed him before the Elamites invaded, ending the First Dynasty. The Elamites ruled Ur until they were overthrown by Sumerian King Eannatum of Lagash, who controlled much of Sumer as head of one of the world's first empires. Ur reestablished self-rule briefly in an obscure Second Dynasty until the Akkadians took over. They were followed by the "barbarian" Gutian nomads of Iran.

After a coalition army of Uruk and Ur expelled the Gutians, Ur-Nammu ushered in Ur's Third Dynasty (2112-2004 BCE). At this time, according to the Torah, the Semitic patriarch Abraham was living in Ur with his father Terah, his half-sister and wife Sarah, and other family members. They migrated north around the time of Ur-Nammu's death in 2096 BCE.

Ur-Nammu unified the southern floodplain cities and gained supremacy over most of Mesopotamia. He reestablished Sumerian as Mesopotamia's official language and initiated astounding building projects around Mesopotamia; his figurines often show him carrying building materials. He built walls around his capital, constructed numerous ziggurats (including the Great Ziggurat of Ur), and more irrigation canals. He also instituted schools to train government officials in cuneiform writing and other skills.

This cylinder-seal impression, circa 2100 BCE, depicts King Ur-Nammu.

Credit: Steve Harris, CC BY-SA 2.0 https://creativecommons.org/licenses/by-sa/2.0 via Wikimedia Commons;
https://commons.wikimedia.org/wiki/File:Sumerian_Cylinder_Seal_of_King_Ur-Nammu.jpg

Ur-Nammu is most famous for writing the first law code that has survived. It covered murder, kidnapping, slave rights, premarital sex, sorcery, and more. If someone accused a person of witchcraft or a husband accused his wife of adultery, they had to endure an ordeal by water.

What was ordeal by water? The tablets didn't say, but the Torah and the Code of Hammurabi give some clues. The Torah stipulated that if a man suspected his wife of adultery but had no proof, the priest would give her holy water mixed with a sprinkling of dust from the tabernacle floor. If nothing happened when she drank it, she was innocent. But if she were impure, her belly would swell, her thigh would shrivel, and she would be unable to conceive children (Numbers 5:11-31). Hammurabi said that if someone were accused of a crime with no hard evidence, they could jump into the river. If they drowned, they were guilty, and if they survived, they were innocent. Perhaps one of these "water tests" was similar to Ur-Nammu's ordeal by water.

At the end of Ur-Nammu's reign, Ur was the largest city globally, with approximately sixty-five thousand people. Ur-Nammu's son Shulgi succeeded him; a hymn recounts his incredulous achievement of running one hundred miles from Nippur to Ur in one day. And yes, that can be done! Today, ultra-distance runners can run one hundred miles (on level ground) in about twenty hours, but an elite runner can complete that distance in eleven hours. Whether Shulgi actually ran that distance or hopped in a chariot once he was out of sight of the cities is another question.

Shulgi built a remarkable 155-mile-long wall to keep the Amorites out of Sumer, which his descendants maintained and reinforced. However, it failed to protect Sumer from a 1940 BCE invasion from the southeast. The Elamites simply went around the end of the wall, got into Sumer, sacked Ur, and captured the king. Ur never regained political power, but its access to the Persian Gulf and the Euphrates enabled the city to continue as a vital trade conduit for the next thousand years.

The Amorites of Babylonia, the Akkadian Sealand dynasty, the Kassites, the Elamites, and the Assyrians ruled Ur successively during the next millennia. Ur declined after Babylon fell to the Persians in 530 BCE. The city lost its entire population when the Euphrates shifted west, which caused its outlet to the Persian Gulf to silt over.

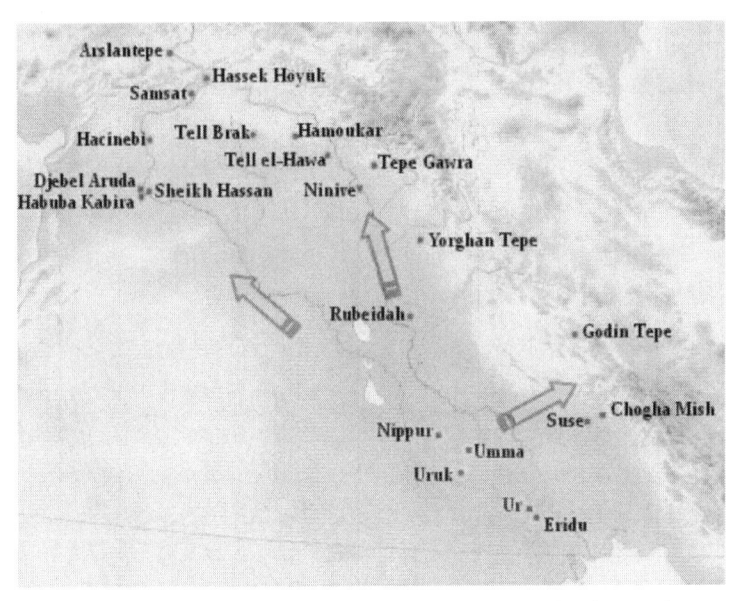

Uruk controlled Mesopotamian cities hundreds of miles north.

Credit: Middle_East_topographic_map-blank.svg: Sémhur (talk)derivative work: Zunkir - This file was derived from: Middle East topographic map-blank.svg:, CC BY-SA 3.0 https://creativecommons.org/licenses/by-sa/3.0 via Wikimedia Commons; https://commons.wikimedia.org/w/index.php?curid=25540654

Uruk was a key city, the dominant city for a time, in ancient Mesopotamia. It was located about forty miles north of Ur on the east bank of the Euphrates. The *Sumerian King List* names King Enmerkar as its founder around 4500 BCE, although archaeological evidence shows an Ubaid settlement dating to about 5000 BCE. The Torah (Genesis 10:10) identifies Uruk as ruled by the mighty warrior and hunter Nimrod. The *Epic of Gilgamesh* says Gilgamesh built Uruk's walls and ruled the city in the 27th century BCE.

Although Eridu was established hundreds of years earlier, Uruk was Mesopotamia's powerhouse for 1,600 years until Ur rose to preeminence. At its peak, Uruk had an astonishing population of forty thousand inside the city walls and eighty thousand people in its immediate area. It was probably the largest city in the world around 3100 BCE. Uruk had an organized military, full-time civil servants, and a stratified society.

Archaeologists believe Uruk was the first city to build immense stone or brick structures, including the first ziggurat. It was the first to mass-produce beveled-rim pottery bowls, and its people invented the cylinder seal, which was rolled in soft clay to produce pictures and written characters. It may have been where the first writing was devised (if not Eridu). The entrancing Lady of Warka mask (Warka is another name for Uruk) is the first preserved depiction of a human face. It perhaps is a sculpture of Uruk's patron goddess Inanna.

The Lady of Warka mask dates to about 3100 BCE in Uruk.
Credit: Osama Shukir Muhammed Amin FRCP(Glasg), CC BY-SA 4.0
https://creativecommons.org/licenses/by-sa/4.0 via Wikimedia
Commons;https://commons.wikimedia.org/wiki/File:Warka_mask_(cropped).jpg

The extraordinary Uruk period, spanning from 4100 to 2900 BCE, saw a rapid expansion of cities in southern Mesopotamia, of which Uruk was the trade and administrative hub. Uruk had a wall around its perimeter, supposedly built by the great Gilgamesh, but it also had an interior wall dividing the newer Eanna district from the older Anu district. Like Eridu, Uruk had an elaborate irrigation system, producing an agricultural surplus of domestic grain.

After 2900 BCE, Uruk faded somewhat in power and population; however, it continued as a city long after Eridu and Ur dissolved into oblivion. Although it declined in prestige and people after Eridu and Ur were abandoned in the 6th century BCE, Uruk's fascinating 5,200-year history of inhabitation continued until 700 CE. By that time, the Euphrates had changed course, leaving Uruk in the middle of a bleak desert. The shifting sands quickly covered the abandoned city, hiding its mysteries until the mid-1850s when British archaeologist William Loftus rediscovered it.

The Neo-Sumerian civilization declined and finally collapsed in 2004 BCE, and within two centuries, Sumerian was a dead spoken language. However, the Sumerian language continued in written literary works and religious liturgy, and the brilliant Sumerian culture exercised considerable influence over the Assyrian and Babylonian civilizations. The Akkadians and fierce Amorites swept into the land between the rivers, synthesizing their language and culture with the Sumerians' ways.

What, specifically, was the Sumerian legacy? Where do we start? The enthralling Sumerians instituted the first schools to teach the first written language, with which they wrote the first law code and epic poetry. They also used it to keep track of administrative affairs. They ingeniously developed the concept of time, creating the sixty-second minute and the sixty-minute hour. They divided day and night into twelve-hour periods and instituted a workday time limit and days off for holidays.

The Sumerians astutely developed measurements around 4000 BCE, which led to the rise of arithmetic, algebra, and geometry. They were the first to build large buildings, like ziggurats, from stone or brick and the first to build empires. They invented the sailboat, initiated large-scale pottery production, and developed metallurgy. They invented the wheel, created the arch, and were the first to have irrigated fields and cultivate grain on a large scale to make bread. And that led to beer! Let's not forget beer!

Chapter 3 – Sargon of Akkad: The First Ruler

From mysterious origins, Sargon the Great rose to establish the world's first multi-ethnic empire with a central government. Through subterfuge and switching alliances, he conquered Kish and Uruk, then continued brazenly expanding his massive empire to include all of Mesopotamia and parts of Anatolia (Turkey), Elam (western Iran), and Syria. Reigning from 2334 to 2279 BCE, Sargon founded the first Semitic dynasty, known as the Sargonic or Old Akkadian dynasty.

Some scholars equate Sargon with the exceptional warrior Nimrod, a distant descendent of Noah who built a massive empire in Shinar (Sumer), then expanded north. According to the Torah, "The first centers of his kingdom were Babylonia, Uruk, Akkad and Kalneh in Shinar. From that land he went to Assyria, where he built Nineveh, Rehoboth Ir, Calah, and Resen" (Genesis 10). Where was Akkad, and who were the Akkadians?

Akkad (Agade) most likely existed before Sargon; perhaps he enlarged a village into a city or restored an older city. In the early 3rd millennium, the Semitic Akkadian tribes began settling in central and southern Mesopotamia after migrating from the Arabian

Peninsula. Akkad's location is a mystery; its ruins lay undiscovered under the desert's shifting sands, presumably along the Tigris or Euphrates somewhere north of Uruk.

The Akkadian language, the earliest documented Semitic language, preceded Sargon. The language first appeared in its written form in the mid-3rd millennium, borrowing from the Sumerian cuneiform script. A bowl discovered in Ur has an inscription in Akkadian from Queen Gan-saman (probably from Akkad) to her husband King Meskiagnunna (circa 2485-2450), about a century before Sargon's rise to power.

Most of us are familiar with the baby Moses drifting in a basket down the Nile to be found by the pharaoh's daughter or the twin newborns Romulus and Remus floating down the Tiber in a basket to be found by a she-wolf. In a 7th-century BCE Neo-Assyrian text, Sargon described his origins:

> "Sargon, the mighty king, king of Agade, am I. My mother was a changeling; I didn't know my father. The brother(s) of my father loved the hills. My home was in the highlands, where the herbs grow on the banks of the Euphrates.
>
> My mother conceived me in secret; she gave birth to me in concealment. She set me in a basket of rushes; she sealed my lid with bitumen. She cast me into the river, but it did not rise over me.
>
> The water carried me to Akki, the drawer of water. He lifted me out as he dipped his jar into the river. Akki took me as his son; he raised me and made me his gardener. While I was a gardener, Ishtar granted me her love."

When Sargon referred to his mother as a "changeling," he might have been referring to the androgynous nature of the priests/priestesses of Inanna (Ishtar). In other traditions, Sargon's mother was a high-priestess (or cult prostitute) of Inanna. She had to hide her apparently illegitimate pregnancy and birth, so she sent him down the river. Sargon said the goddess Ishtar visited him as a youth, inspiring him to rise to greatness.

The goddess Inanna (Ishtar) rests her foot on a lion on this cylindrical seal.
https://commons.wikimedia.org/wiki/File:Ancient_Akkadian_Cylindrical_Seal_Depicting_Inanna_and_Ninshubur.jpg

Akki, Sargon's adopted father, made Sargon his gardener; most likely, Akki was a palace gardener and trained Sargon in the art. According to the *Sumerian King List*, Kish was the first city built after the Great Flood, and it was located in northern Sumer. Sargon somehow rose to the position of cupbearer to King Ur-Zababa, a remarkable feat for a foundling child and palace gardener. A cupbearer was a trusted official who protected the king from poison and was his confidante and informal advisor.

One day, Sargon had an appalling vision: the goddess Inanna (Ishtar) told him she was planning to drown King Ur-Zababa in a river of blood. As he dreamed, Sargon groaned and gnashed his teeth in horror. Hearing of this, the king called Sargon to him, demanding that he reveal his dream. What Sargon told him was frightening. The king bit his lip in fear, certain that Sargon aspired to usurp his throne and assassinate him. He had to kill Sargon before Sargon could kill him!

King Ur-Zababa sent Sargon with his bronze mirror to the chief smith, Beliš-Tikal, supposedly to repair it. But Ur-Zababa had secretly ordered Beliš-Tikal to throw Sargon into the statue mold so he would be covered with molten metal! Everyone would think his dead body was a metal figurine. But the goddess Inanna intervened, ordering Sargon not to enter the gates of the smith's house. The king paled in fear when Sargon later showed up at the palace, healthy and whole.

With his murderous plot foiled, the king had to find another way to eliminate his would-be assassin. Then, he heard his great enemy, King Lugal-Zage-Si of Umma, was approaching Kish after systematically conquering the other city-states of Sumer, uniting them into one Sumerian empire. After taking Uruk, he marched toward Kish in the far north of Sumer. King Ur-Zababa was worried when he heard Lugal-Zage-Si was heading his way. But could he somehow work this to his advantage?

He sent Sargon to Lugal-Zage-Si with a clay tablet, ostensibly suing for peace. But the secret message on the tablet asked Lugal-Zage-Si to kill Sargon. After reading the tablet, Lugal-Zage-Si looked at Sargon and chuckled. Why would he kill this man when he could use him? After all, he was the king's cupbearer; he had inside information! Lugal-Zage-Si invited Sargon to join forces with him. Sargon accepted, and together, they successfully attacked Kish. Ur-Zababa fled.

This bronze mask, possibly of Sargon, might be the world's first depiction of a man-bun.

https://commons.wikimedia.org/wiki/File:Sargon_of_Akkad_(1936).jpg

It wasn't long, however, before Sargon and Lugal-Zage-Si had a falling out. Rumors that Sargon was sleeping with the king's wife enraged Lugal-Zage-Si, and the two allies became sworn enemies. Sargon attacked Uruk and tore down its walls. Lugal-Zage-Si rushed to defend the city he'd only recently taken for himself, but Sargon defeated him in battle, dragging him in chains with a yoke on his neck to Nippur, the sacred sanctuary of the god Enlil. This was the god that Lugal-Zage-Si had always called upon. Sargon forced him to walk in humiliation through Nippur's gate before proclaiming himself king of Kish with Ishtar as his patron goddess.

Sargon had this inscription carved into a statue's pedestal in the temple of Enlil:

> "Sargon, king of Akkad, overseer of Inanna, king of Kish, anointed of Anu, king of the land, governor of Enlil. He defeated the city of Uruk and tore down its walls; in the battle of Uruk, he won, took Lugal-Zage-Si, king of Uruk, in the course of the battle and led him in a collar to the gate of Enlil."

By defeating Lugal-Zage-Si, Sargon nominally inherited all the city-states of Sumer that Lugal-Zage-Si had conquered and formed into one unified Sumerian state. And it was not just Sumer; the ambitious Lugal-Zage-Si had pressed west as far as the Mediterranean! Of course, assuming control over Lugal-Zage-Si's former mini-empire was not an easy matter. Most Sumerian cities were reluctant to submit to a new overlord, especially one that wasn't even Sumerian. One by one, Sargon had to retake the Sumerian cities.

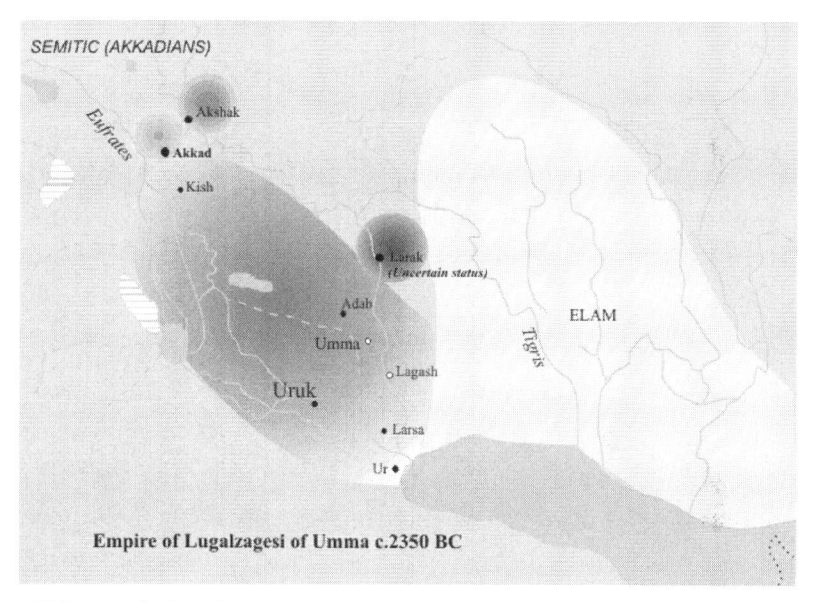

This map depicts the area Lugal-Zage-Si controlled and a possible location of Akkad.

Credit: CC BY-SA 3.0, https://commons.wikimedia.org/w/index.php?curid=1084105

Sargon also had to prove his legitimacy. He had no known royal heritage, and his birth was mysterious and likely illegitimate. Abandoned by unknown parents, he labored as a gardener until he was abruptly raised to be the king's cupbearer; he then turned on that king (admittedly in self-defense) and forcibly stole his throne. He renamed himself Sargon or Sharrukin (Akkadian for "legitimate king"); we have no idea what his original name was. He had to vigorously promote his right to rule by reminding everyone of Ishtar's favor and the support of the god Enlil and other deities.

"Sargon, king of Agade, was victorious over Ur in battle, conquered the city and destroyed its wall. He conquered Eninmar, destroyed its walls, and conquered its district and Lagash as far as the sea. He washed his weapons in the sea. He was victorious over Umma in battle. The god Enlil made Sargon the unrivaled lord of the land and gave him the Upper and Lower Sea."

(Inscription of Sargon, Old Babylonian copy from Nippur)

Once Sumer's cities capitulated to Sargon's control, he turned north to open trade routes and control sources of silver and other riches. He conquered his way up the Euphrates to Syria and then northeast to Anatolia and its silver-rich mountains. He took Susa, the Elamite capital in the Zagros Mountains (today's Iran).

An epic tale preserved in the Hittite and Akkadian manuscripts called *King of Battle* tells how some Akkadian merchants in Buru Shanda (Purshahanda) in Anatolia asked him to arbitrate a regional dispute with the oppressive ruler Nur-Dagan. In a lightning-fast attack, Sargon literally brought Nur-Dagan to his knees, and Buru Shanda came under Akkadian control.

Although the goddess Ishtar (Inanna) was Sargon's first patroness, he later began worshiping the Semitic god Dagan, who is often equated with the Mesopotamian god Enlil, whom Sargon considered a patron or supporter-champion. Dagan, the father of the god Baal, was a deity of the Syrians and the middle region of Mesopotamia (including Akkad). Dagan later became the god of the Philistines in Canaan. The Mesopotamians considered Dagan capable of granting kingship, and Sargon desired all the legitimacy he could acquire.

After bowing to Dagan, Sargon overcame northern Mesopotamia and the Levant (modern-day western Turkey, Syria, Lebanon, Jordan, Israel, and Palestine). He also invaded Canaan and Syria four times, up to Lebanon's cedar forest. According to the *King of*

Battle, he set sail across the Mediterranean, arriving in Kuppara, which was probably Crete or Cyprus. Sargon ruled a vast empire from the "Upper Sea" (the Mediterranean) to the "Lower Sea" (the Persian Gulf).

In 1867 CE, archaeologist Sir Henry Rawlinson unearthed the Library of Ashurbanipal while excavating the ancient Assyrian city of Nineveh. He found the *Legend of Sargon* in the library, which is purportedly Sargon's autobiography. Sargon speaks of an uprising during his "old age."

> "In my old age of 55, all the lands revolted against me, and they besieged me in Agade [Akkad], but the old lion still had teeth and claws. I went forth to battle and defeated them: I knocked them over and destroyed their vast army. Now, any king who wants to call himself my equal, wherever I went, let him go!"

Sargon's principal wife was Queen Tashlultum, and his daughter Enheduanna was a powerful priestess who composed hymns, including the *Exaltation of Inanna*, which was sung by devotees of Inanna (Ishtar) for centuries. Sargon's son Rimush succeeded him as king, and another son, Manishtushu, assumed the throne after Rimush's courtiers murdered him. Sargon had at least two more sons: Shu-Enlil and Ilaba'is-takal.

This Akkadian cylinder seal depicts a hunting scene. It is dated to about 2250 BCE.

Credit: Metropolitan Museum of Art, CC0, via Wikimedia Commons; https://commons.wikimedia.org/wiki/File:Akkadian_cylinder_seal_and_modern_impression_hunting_scene_ca_2250_2150_BC.jpg

To maintain the lands he had conquered, Sargon organized a well-structured bureaucracy. He astutely placed his finest and most dependable Akkadian administrators, known as the "Citizens of Akkad," as city leaders and provincial governors throughout his empire. He ingeniously placed his daughter Enheduanna in Ur as the high priestess of Inanna, where she engineered religious and cultural affairs in the southern regions.

Sargon did not dismantle the Sumerian religion; he actually embraced it. But he did make the Akkadian language the official administrative language of his empire, although he used Sumerian cuneiform for its script. Most Sumerians were probably bilingual in both Akkadian and Sumerian. He unified his realm by placing Akkadian as the lingua franca (common language to all).

By controlling such a large region of the known world, Sargon promoted trade throughout today's Middle Eastern countries. The cedars of Lebanon and the silver of Anatolia provided treasures in raw goods. His trade routes extended to the Indus Valley (modern-day Pakistan and northern India) and the regions around the Persian Gulf (modern-day Saudi Arabia, the United Arab Emirates, Oman, and Iran). He traded wool and olive oil for India's pearls and ivory, the lapis lazuli of Badakhshān (northeastern

Afghanistan), and Anatolia's copper, silver, and other precious metals. Sargon taxed the merchants to support his military, scribes, and royal artists.

After sensationally conquering what he called the "four corners of the universe," Sargon's military forces and administrators maintained peace and order throughout his empire. This stability enabled road construction, enhanced irrigation projects, extensive trade, and astounding developments in the sciences and arts. Using the Akkadian language in cuneiform script, the clay tablets and cylinder seals of Sargon's era display an innovative spirit of calligraphy with exquisite scenes depicting festivals and mythology.

The first postal system emerged in the Akkadian Empire; these were outer clay envelopes encircling clay tablets with cuneiform messages. The sender inscribed the name and address of the recipient on the outer clay envelope and pressed his or her official seal on it. The only way to open the clay envelope was to break it, thus preserving the message inside for the person meant to read it and no one else.

According to the *Sumerian King List*, Sargon ruled for fifty-five years. But was he a good or a bad emperor? Did he deserve the nomenclature "Sargon the Great?" He was great in the sense that he conquered an incredible section of the known world and organized it into a stable, relatively peaceful empire. He ensured the ease of trade, allowed the arts and sciences to flourish, and oversaw a secure, affluent, orderly, and progressive society for his citizens. Accounts of his life say he protected the weak, the widows, and the orphans. Apparently, everyone had enough to eat in Sumer; no one needed to beg for food.

The Mesopotamians called Sargon's reign their golden age in the centuries following his death. He enriched his empire with widespread trade, bringing precious goods and raw materials from distant lands, and he enlightened the provinces he ruled by spreading vast amounts of knowledge. The Sumerians had previously developed mathematical and scientific understandings; they experienced further breakthroughs since Sargon encouraged scholarly studies and the interchange of ideas with other lands. Sculptures, paintings, mosaics, metallurgy, and architecture rose to new heights once various cultures shared their techniques and styles.

Yet, especially in his later years, incessant rebellions rocked Sargon's empire, which, in his own words, were met by "a lion with teeth and claws." What caused the uprisings? No literature or inscriptions survive that portray him as unjust. Yes, he was harsh if cities resisted being conquered by him, and he was ruthless when suppressing uprisings. But once Sargon established peace and justice, his rule was relatively benign. The rebellions do not appear to be racially motivated; the Sumerians did not seem to take issue with him being a Semite.

His biographers said the problem was spiritual, attributing the revolts to the anger of the god Marduk and "because of the evil which he had committed." The specific evil has not been identified. Perhaps the god was angry about all the violence involved in conquering nations. Maybe he was vexed by the abuses of justice (Marduk was the god of fairness and truth). According to *The Curse of Agade*, written two centuries later, Marduk also brought a famine that destroyed Sargon's people.

At any rate, Sargon marched out to meet his mutinous aggressors, turning the rebel city of Kassala into heaps of ruins and leaving no tree or building for a bird to rest. He attacked Subartu (northern Mesopotamia) and overthrew the insurgents, destroying countless combatants, pillaging their city, and bringing the loot back to Akkad.

What was Sargon's legacy? He continued building the empire started by Lugal-Zage-Si, consolidating all of Sumer and then expanding into the Levant and Anatolia. He founded a military tradition that continued through Mesopotamia's history. His half-century reign formed a strong command that stood firm through the rule of his two sons and his remarkable grandson Naram-Sin. Mesopotamian kings regarded him as an exemplary archetype of leadership.

Chapter 4 – Akkad: The First Empire

The astounding Akkadian Empire was history's first true multi-ethnic empire with a strong, centralized state. Although "mini-empires" of several city-states had previously existed in Sumer, such as under King Eannatum of Lagash, they were monocultural. They had the same ethnicity, same language, same religion, and same culture. The Akkadian civilization had already begun to flourish in central Mesopotamia's fertile alluvial plain. As Sumer's Early Dynastic period drew to a close, the Akkadian Empire rose to dominate from 2334 to 2154 BCE, coinciding with the Early Bronze Age civilizations in Canaan (Israel), Syria, and Turkey. At its peak, the Akkadian Empire stretched for thousands of miles from the Mediterranean to the Persian Gulf and encompassed numerous ethnic groups and cultures.

The political landscape in the Early Dynastic period had been fragmented, with no lasting central government. Each city-state was like its own small country, although one city would occasionally rise to dominance and exert power over the others for a while. Sumer had been the dominant culture in southern Mesopotamia, and as time passed, Akkadian immigrants from the Arabian Peninsula rose to become the preeminent civilization of middle and northern Mesopotamia. Like the Sumerians, the Akkadians had independent, self-governing city-states but shared a Semitic language, religion, and culture. When Sargon the Great conquered all of Sumer and then the rest of Mesopotamia (and beyond), he brought the Sumerians and Akkadians together under one government and language. He then expanded into Syria, Lebanon, Canaan, Anatolia (Turkey), and Elam (Iran), forming a multi-cultural empire.

Even before Sargon the Great's stunning empire-building feats, kings with Semitic names ruled Kish, including Ur-Zababa, under whom Sargon had served as cupbearer. But Sargon's fame eclipsed these early Semitic rulers. He raised statues of his image along the Mediterranean to celebrate his victories in Canaan and Syria. He also brought home spoils from his conquests to adorn his palaces and temples. He campaigned to the west, subduing the Elamites and contending with King Sarlak of Gutium.

This scene is a segment of the Victory Stele of Rimush over Lagash.

Credit: Louvre Museum, CC BY 3.0 https://creativecommons.org/licenses/by/3.0 via Wikimedia Commons; https://commons.wikimedia.org/wiki/File:P1150890_Louvre_st%C3%A8le_de_victoire_Akkad_AO2678_rwk.jpg

Sargon the Great ruled from 2334 to his death in 2279 BCE, after which his son Rimush ascended the throne as the second ruler of the Akkadian Empire. Rimush reigned for nine turbulent years, struggling to hold the empire together as numerous revolts broke out in Ur, Umma, Adab, Lagash, Der, and Kassala. In response to the Sumerian uprisings, he ruthlessly annihilated enormous numbers of people and uprooted the cities' foundations.

In three merciless battles against rebel princes in Sumer, he killed fifty-six thousand people, enslaved over twenty-nine thousand, and sent over twenty-five thousand into exile. The 6 cities lost a shocking total of about 111,000 people to the mass slaughter; this was most of their population! He parceled out the agricultural lands around the vanquished cities to the Akkadian Empire's new land-holding class. The few survivors of the massacres had no legal right to farm their ancestral lands.

Rimush destroyed Sumerian cities and even his own Akkadian cities, including Kassala on the Euphrates River between Kish and Akkad. Sargon had already flattened Kassala following an earlier revolt. After rebuilding, they challenged Rimush, who retaliated by killing twelve thousand Akkadian rebel soldiers, enslaving five thousand citizens, and leveling the city to the ground a second time.

Rimush's own officials assassinated him in 2270 BCE, bashing him to death with their marble or metal cylinder seals. Perhaps the atrocities against the fellow Akkadian city of Kassala were too much for his people to endure. It's likely some of his officials hailed from Kassala. Even if not, they probably thought that decimating the empire's population was not the way to go. No doubt, his officials worried that the constant instability would disrupt the empire's lucrative trade. It is possible Rimush's brother Manishtushu was plotting against him, desiring a return to stability.

Manishtushu assumed the throne upon his brother's death and ruled for fourteen years. The *Sumerian King List* said he was the older brother of Rimush. Why wasn't he king first before his brother then? Some scholars theorize the two were twins. Others speculate that Sargon may have selected Rimush as his successor, feeling that Rimush had a more resolute character and could manage rebellions better.

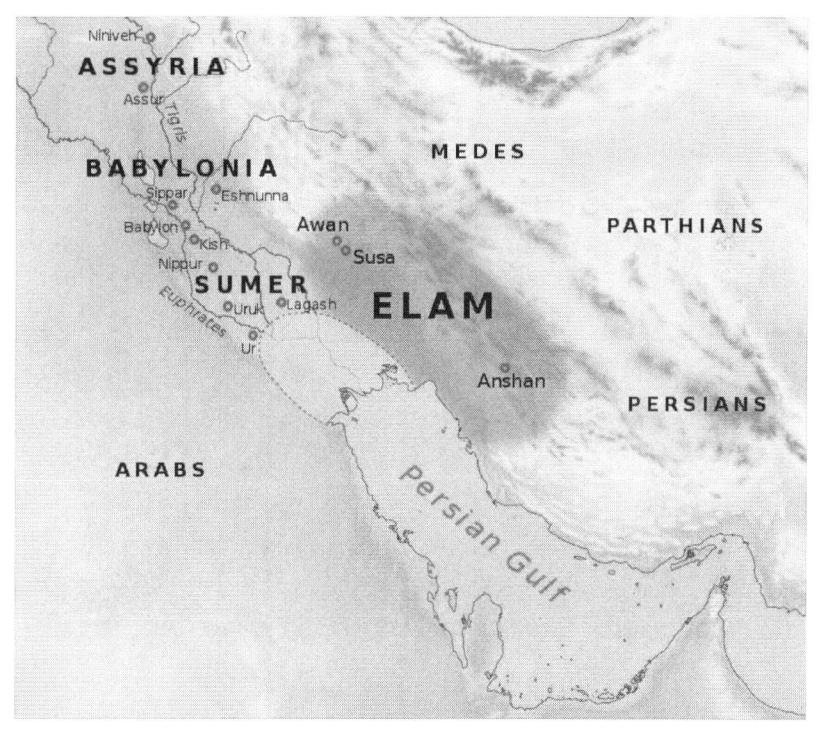

This map depicts the regions around the Persian Gulf that Manishtushu controlled and shows how far the Persian Gulf extended into Mesopotamia in the Bronze Age.

Credit: File:Near East topographic map-blank.svg: SémhurFile:Elam-map-PL.svg: Wkotwicaderivative work: Morningstar1814 - File:Elam-map-PL.svg, CC BY-SA 3.0, https://creativecommons.org/licenses/by-sa/3.0 via Wikimedia Commons; https://commons.wikimedia.org/w/index.php?curid=61956849

Because Rimush had ferociously squelched insurgencies within the empire, Manishtushu could focus on regions outside the empire's borders. He launched ambitious military campaigns to expand Akkadian territory and strategically enhanced trade relations with foreign civilizations. He sailed a fleet around the Persian Gulf, gathering a coalition of thirty-two kings through conquest or alliances to commandeer trade in the coastal lands. Manishtushu spectacularly invaded Elam via the Persian Gulf, looted its silver mines in Susa, and installed Akkadian governors. He sent his fleet up the Tigris River and traded with thirty-seven other city-states.

Manishtushu erected statues of himself throughout multiple cities under his reign. The images were the same, but the inscriptions honored a different god in each city, as the city-states all had their own patron deity. All the inscriptions lauded his successful overseas expedition around the Persian Gulf, an accomplishment that must have made him exceptionally proud. He also might have been exercising diplomacy. While Sargon's and Rimush's statues touted their violent repression of local insurgencies, Manishtushu focused on military successes overseas that had enriched Akkad and Sumer.

Like his brother, Manishtushu fell victim to palace intrigue. For unclear reasons, his officials assassinated him, and his son, Naram-Sin, ascended the throne as the fourth king of the Akkadian Empire. Naram-Sin sprang to greatness much as his grandfather Sargon had. He took the empire to exceptional heights in his thirty-sixth regnal year. During his rule, which lasted from 2254 to 2218 BCE, the Akkadian Empire reached its peak of power.

Naram-Sin picked up where his father had left off with victorious military campaigns in northern Syria and western Iran. He besieged Magan (probably modern-day Oman), taking its king captive. He fought multiple wars against the Armenian (Armeni) people of Ararat in today's eastern Turkey (where the Torah said Noah's ark landed). Like his grandfather, he assumed the title "ruler of the four corners of the universe."

Naram-Sin was not only a military man; he was also astute with financial affairs and standardized his kingdom's accounts. He appointed his daughters as high-priestesses of several important cults in Mesopotamia, which increased the people's acceptance of his dynasty and enhanced his control of the regions they were in.

The Victory Stele of Naram-Sin, now on display in the Louvre Museum in Paris, depicts him as larger than life, towering over other people and wearing a horned helmet, both of which imply divine standing. His admiring citizens deified him, raising him to the status of a living god of Agade (Akkad). And yet, accepting his citizens' adulation offended the gods, according to *The Curse of Agade*, and they poured out their wrath on the empire after Naram-Sin's death.

This cylinder seal impression reads "The Divine Shar-Kali-Sharri, Prince of Akkad."

Credit: Mbzt 2011, CC BY 3.0 https://creativecommons.org/licenses/by/3.0 via Wikimedia Commons; https://commons.wikimedia.org/w/index.php?curid=77501439

After the popular Naram-Sin died, his son, Shar-Kali-Sharri, ascended the throne and ruled for twenty-four years from 2217 to 2193 BCE. He led stellar military campaigns but did not measure up to his father's spectacular reign due to external threats and crippling climate change. The savage Gutian hill tribes had begun sporadically raiding Akkadian territory during Naram-Sin's reign, and they were growing bolder, attacking more frequently and viciously. To support his military campaigns against the Gutians, Shar-Kali-Sharri levied taxes on his vassal city-states, but this led to insurgencies from disgruntled kings. He fortuitously captured Sharlag, King of Gutium, and stymied the Gutian attacks. He waged three successive years of victorious campaigns against the Amorites and fought successfully against the Elamites for two years.

Then, beginning around 2200 BCE, a horrifying drought struck, forcing the populations of some of the hardest-hit areas to abandon their cities for the encroaching desert, migrating in search of more well-watered regions. Seventy-four percent of Mesopotamian settlements lost their population in this catastrophic period. This was more than just a local drought; Egyptian records documented drought in the same period during Pharaoh Pepi's reign.

When Shar-Kali-Sharri died in 2193 BCE, anarchy raised its perilous head. With no clear-cut successor, four would-be emperors wrestled for control while the empire dwindled. As the *Sumerian King List* put it, "Then who was king? Who was not the king? Igigi, Imi, Nanum, Ilulu: four of them ruled for only three years."

As it turned out, none of the four contenders won. Instead, a fifth man, King Dudu, took the throne in 2189 BCE and held it for twenty-one years. But he was only a king, not an emperor; the empire had shrunk down to the city-state of Akkad and several nearby cities. Taking advantage of the instability, the Gutians had made decisive inroads into Mesopotamia during the anarchy period; some scholars even believe that King Ilulu may have been Gutian.

The *Sumerian King List* records that Dudu's son Shu-turul succeeded him in 2168 BCE, ruling as the last-known king of Akkad, Kish, and Eshnunna. Fifteen years later, the Gutians conquered Akkad and ruled over Mesopotamia for half a century. Eventually, a coalition army of Uruk and Ur chased the Gutians out of Sumer, and the Third Dynasty of Ur rose to prominence in 2112.

Who is he? This king's sculpture dates to the Akkadian era, but his identity is unknown.

Credit: Metropolitan Museum of Art, CC0, via Wikimedia Commons; https://commons.wikimedia.org/wiki/File:Head_of_a_ruler_ca_2300_2000_BC_Iran_or_Meso potamia_Metropolitan_Museum_of_Art_(dark_background).jpg

What was the social and political structure of the Akkadian Empire? Like the Sumerians, the Akkadians were polytheistic and worshiped most of the same gods the Sumerians worshiped: An, the sky god; Enlil, the god of air; Nanna, the god of the moon; and Utu, the sun god. They worshiped Inanna, often under the name Ishtar. The Akkadians believed their kings were the earthly representation of the gods. They perceived their gods to have human forms and alternate between being wise, reckless, humorous, or irate; the gods were unconcerned with morality.

Because the Akkadian Empire covered a vast region with multiple ethnicities, it was politically unified, but each area continued with its own culture and social system. However, most of Mesopotamia continued with the social system in place in Sumer. The Akkadians adopted the Sumerian cuneiform script to write the Akkadian language and assiduously recorded, in minute detail, aspects of life in the cities.

The Akkadians had a hierarchical system of five classes: the nobility, priests/priestesses, upper class, lower class, and enslaved people. The nobility included the kings, governors, and other ruling class members and was intricately linked to the priestly class. The kings often appointed their sons to be governors of strategic provinces and their daughters as high priestesses in significant cities. They also married their daughters to rulers of distant regions of the empire. Most conquered cities had both a civil and military administration that ruled parallel with each other. Akkadian troops were stationed in the conquered cities to ensure compliance with their overlords. Akkadian governors replaced most city administrators.

The priests and priestesses commanded profound respect because they could interpret omens and signs. They were literate and served as doctors and dentists in the temples' outer courts. The upper class consisted of wealthy merchants, teachers, scribes, military officers, architects, shipbuilders, and accountants. Only boys attended school, but girls from leading families learned at home from tutors. Sargon's daughter Enheduanna must have learned to read and write since she was a famous hymn-writer.

The lower classes kept the cities fed and operating. This included the farmers, construction workers, basket weavers, fishermen, lower-ranking soldiers, and craftspeople. Men and women could and did climb the social ladder to have an upper-class standing. Women appeared to have a relatively high status, especially in the arena of religion, where they often served as high priestesses. They also served as tavern owners, doctors, and dentists.

This carving shows Akkadian soldiers on Nara-Sim's victory stele, circa 2250 BCE.

Credit: Rama, CC BY-SA 2.0 FR <https://creativecommons.org/licenses/by-sa/2.0/fr/deed.en>, via Wikimedia Commons; https://commons.wikimedia.org/wiki/File:Akkadian_Empire_soldiers_on_the_victory_stele_of_Naram-Sin_circa_2250_BC.jpg

Most enslaved people were war captives, but a person could sell themselves or their children into slavery to pay a debt or receive enslavement as punishment for a crime. Slaves came from all ethnicities, including Akkadian, and had wide-ranging responsibilities depending on their skills and education. They were not only manual laborers; they also worked as estate managers, tutors, accountants, and craftspeople. They could buy or earn their freedom.

Trade capabilities for the Akkadian Empire were rich and varied. The Persian Gulf and the Euphrates and Tigris Rivers served as the empire's water highways. From the Persian Gulf, the

Akkadians sailed into the Arabian Sea to India. A network of unpaved roads connected Akkad with its far-flung empire. Camel caravans carried goods and people over desert terrain, and mules and donkeys pulled carts and sleds. They even had a postal service!

Their trade routes extended to the silver, tin, and copper mines of Anatolia, Lebanon's cedar forests, and the lapis lazuli mines of Bactria (Afghanistan). The Akkadians had an abundant and varied food supply, thanks to irrigation techniques learned from the Sumerians. Since they usually had a surplus, they could trade grain, dried fish, and dried fruit for resources they did not have, such as lumber, metal ore, and stone for construction.

The Akkadian Empire only lasted about 180 years. What factors influenced its downfall? Climate change drastically impacted the empire's decline, which the Akkadians and other Mesopotamians believed resulted from divine retribution. They felt the gods were offended that King Naram-Sin had accepted and promoted being called a living god by his adoring citizens. The gods punished his excessive pride by wreaking devastation on his descendants, which led to poor harvests and food shortages.

Soil analysis of Akkadian sites in northern Mesopotamia indicates a severe drought began around 2200 BCE and endured for three centuries. Archaeological excavations reveal the sudden abandonment of multiple Akkadian cities in Mesopotamia's northern plains, as well as a southern migration. Scientists attributed the devastating drought to erratic weather patterns due to changing wind currents and a horrific volcanic eruption in Anatolia to the north. The Mesopotamian drought was part of the 4.2-kiloyear BP aridification event that lasted from 2200 to 2000 BCE. It was one of the most severe climate changes in human history, and it caused the collapse of empires in Egypt, Mesopotamia, and even China.

After King Shar-Kali-Sharri's death, a power struggle rocked the empire. Several southern Mesopotamian city-states reasserted their independence, causing the empire's borders to deteriorate. The rapacious Gutian tribes swarmed from the Zagros Mountains (in today's Iraq, Iran, and southern Turkey) in increasing numbers, leaving behind devastation in the regions of Akkad, Sumer, and Elam.

As the Akkadian Empire diminished, the nomadic Gutians took advantage of its weakness to launch a decades-long campaign of incessant guerilla attacks, crippling the empire's economy. They disrupted trade through disastrous strikes on camel caravans. Farmers were terrified of working in their fields, as they were afraid the raiding bands would target them. Climate change had already created crushing food shortages; now, the people sank into dire famine conditions.

Around 2100 BCE, the Third Dynasty of Ur, the "Sumerian Renaissance," rose to preeminence in Mesopotamia, shifting power from Akkad back to the southern regions of Sumer. This shift created a return to the Sumerian language for general communication; however, a modified form of Akkadian continued for the next millennia as the trade and diplomatic language of Mesopotamia. Eventually, the Babylonian language replaced both languages in 1000 BCE.

The Akkadians were astute assimilators but not the inventors and innovators that the Sumerians were. However, the Akkadian Empire served as a vital bridge between the Sumerian culture and other cultures of the Akkadians' far-reaching empire. They incorporated and shared the Sumerian culture throughout the Middle East while learning from the social organization and commercial practices of the regions they conquered. They were the first "melting pot" of civilization.

PART TWO: Age of Empires (2000–539 BCE)

Chapter 5 – Assyria: An Overview

Creators of the largest empire in the known world at that point, the Assyrians struck fear into other nations for centuries. Their siege engines grounded their enemies' walls into dust, and they displaced entire populations. At its height, the Assyrian Empire stretched from northern Africa (Libya and Egypt), up the eastern Mediterranean coast, including Israel, Lebanon, and Syria, into Anatolia (Turkey), present-day Armenia, and Azerbaijan, down through Mesopotamia, and east into part of modern-day Iran.

Who were the Assyrians, and what were their origins? These fierce empire-builders were originally Semitic pastoral herders living in the city-state of Aššur (Ashur) in today's northern Iraq. The Torah identifies Aššur as being on the western banks of the Tigris River and the man Ashur as the son of Shem and grandson of Noah. The Assyrians worshiped a god named Ashur, who was originally the local deity of the city of Aššur and later their supreme god and national patron. The Assyrians were probably distant relatives of the Akkadians since they spoke the same language. The Torah identifies the Assyrians as being distantly related to the Aramaeans and Hebrews.

Ashur is depicted in this Assyrian "feather-robed archer" figure.
https://commons.wikimedia.org/wiki/File:Ashur_god.jpg

When did the Assyrians rule in Mesopotamia and beyond? Its two-thousand-year history spanned from the Early Bronze Age to the Late Iron Age. Historians usually divide Assyria's history into several segments, beginning with the Early Period (2500-2025 BCE), during which the Akkadian Empire conquered Assyria under Sargon the Great. Nomadic shepherds settled the area of Aššur as early as 2600 BCE, and the nation (and eventually the empire) of Assyria continued until 609 BCE.

After the fall of the Akkadian Empire, the Assyrians rose to power with their own empires, achieving astounding heights in cultural and technological achievements. Their three empires were the Old Assyrian Empire (2025-1522 BCE), the Middle Assyrian Empire (1392-1056 BCE), and Assyria's peak of power in the Neo-Assyrian Empire (911-609 BCE).

Aššur grew into a city-state during the Sumerian period of dominance in Mesopotamia. The early settlers were nomads. The *Assyrian King List* named their oldest known king, Tudiya, as "the first of seventeen kings living in tents." Several other Akkadian-speaking city-states arose in northern Mesopotamia near Aššur:

Nineveh, Gasur, and Arbela. This region was Assyria proper; it was called *Subartu* by the Sumerians and *Azuhinum* by the Akkadians.

When Sargon incorporated Assyria into the Akkadian Empire (2334-2154 BCE), he made Aššur the administrative center of Assyria. In the early Akkadian Empire period, the Assyrians established trading posts with the Hittites in Anatolia (Turkey). Assyria was one of the regions that rebelled against Sargon the Great in his later years, but he brutally counterattacked and subdued them.

After the Akkadian Empire fell, Assyria became fully independent between 2154 to 2112 BCE. The Gutians invaded and occupied central and southern Mesopotamia, but Assyria never fell under their power. When the Third Dynasty of Ur (the Neo-Sumerian Empire) rose to power in 2112 BCE, Ur extended its rule up to Aššur but did not go as far north as Nineveh. The Assyrians ruled Aššur and other cities under Neo-Sumerian dominance as *shakkanakka*, or vassal governors, for Ur until 2080 BCE, when King Ushpia became Assyria's independent ruler.

Several independent kings ruled Assyria until King Puzur-Ashur I ascended the throne, ushering in the Old Assyrian Empire (2025-1522 BCE). Under his reign, Assyria began expanding its trade colonies in Hittite and Hurrian lands in Turkey. Puzur-Ashur's descendant, King Ilu-Shuma (1995-1974 BCE), engaged in military actions in Sumer, freeing Akkadian settlements from Elamite and Amorite oppressors. Ilu-Shuma built the first temple of Ishtar in Aššur.

King Erishum I (1973-1934 BCE) followed Ilu-Shuma; this indomitable king ruled for forty years and wrote one of the earliest legal codes (he came after Ur-Nammu but before Hammurabi or Moses). Assyria's eighteen trading centers in Anatolia traded in bronze, copper, gold, iron, silver, tin, lapis lazuli, grain, and textiles during his reign. He built a temple for the god Ashur, with two beer vats in its courtyard, and a temple for Ishtar and Adad, the Amorite god of rain.

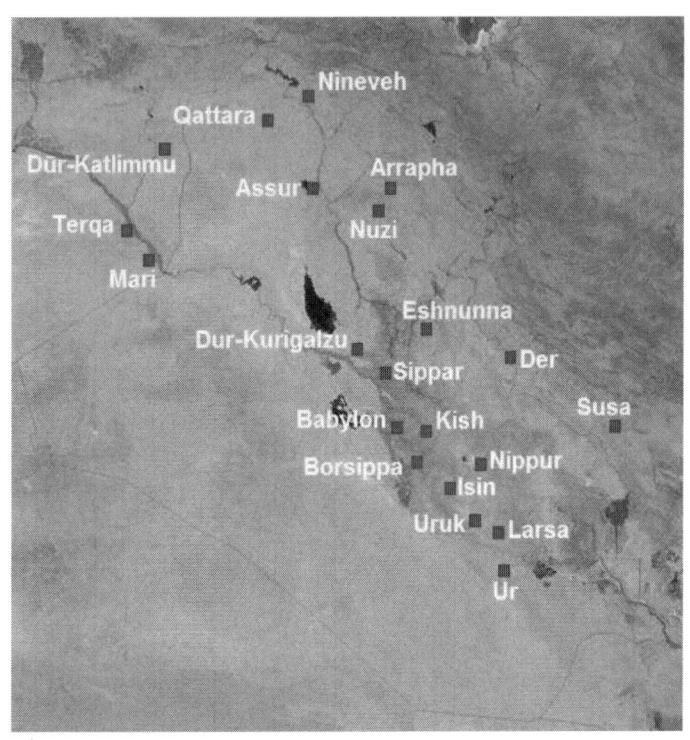

This map shows the major cities of Mesopotamia in the 2^{d} millennium BCE.
Credit: CC BY-SA 2.5; https://commons.wikimedia.org/w/index.php?curid=18438114

In 1808 BCE, Shamshi-Adad, ruler of Terga, usurped the Assyrian throne, overthrowing Puzur-Ashur I's dynasty. He claimed lineage from King Ushpia, but the Assyrians considered him an Amorite. Interestingly, a 2013 DNA analysis of four people's teeth buried in Terga during this era carried haplotypes from the Indian subcontinent. Shamshi-Adad may have been neither Amorite nor Assyrian but rather Mitanni, a people from the north. The Mitanni elite had Indo-Aryan names and worshiped Hindu gods, but the common people spoke the Hurrian language of the Armenian highlands. Apparently, a tribe from the Indian subcontinent had assimilated with the Hurrians but held upper-class status.

Shamshi-Adad was a dynamic leader. He expanded the Assyrian Empire from a small group of city-states to encompass all of northern Mesopotamia and a large swathe of today's Turkey, Syria, Lebanon, and Canaan (Israel). His son, King Ishme-Dagan (1775–1763 BCE), could not hold on to Sumer or the Mediterranean region, although he was a fierce warrior, one "not afraid to risk his own skin." He held a tenuous relationship with King Hammurabi, who was rapidly turning obscure Babylon into a formidable power; Assyria and Babylon were allies at times but also competitors for dominance.

Babylon won the race for power, at least temporarily. The subsequent three Assyrian kings were Babylon's vassals during Hammurabi's long reign. But after Hammurabi's death, Puzur-Sin, an Assyrian vice-regent, threw off the shackles of Babylon, returning Assyria to self-rule by a series of usurpers. The seventh contender for the Assyrian crown, Adasi, "son of nobody," ascended the throne, bringing stability and ending Babylonian and Amorite control.

His successors, the Adaside dynasty, continued to rule Assyria independently. They gradually grew in strength and led Assyria through several peaceful, prosperous centuries. When the Hittites attacked and sacked Babylon, Assyria serenely stood firm. When the Kassites conquered Babylon in 1594 BCE, Assyria was impregnable, calmly upgrading its infrastructure and building temples.

Assyria's strength, stability, and prosperity were interrupted when Egypt enlisted help in a power play against Mitanni. Egypt was concerned about Mitanni's bourgeoning power. They were building their own vast empire that stretched along the Fertile Crescent, from the Mediterranean Levant (Canaan, Lebanon, and Syria) to Anatolia and down into Mesopotamia. Pharaoh Amenhotep II sent King Ashur-nadin-ahhe of Assyria gold in exchange for allying with Egypt against the Mitanni-Hurrians, who had extended their empire down to Egypt's border and were claiming Egypt's tributary cities in the Levant.

Hearing of the alliance, King Shaushtatar of Mitanni allied with the Hittites and launched a preemptive strike on Assyria. They sacked Aššur and made Assyria a vassal state. But similar to their experience with Babylon, the Assyrians survived with their monarchy intact and minimal Mitanni interference for the reign of three Assyrian kings. In less than two decades, Assyria was independent of Mitanni. King Ashur-bel-nisheshu of Assyria (r. 1417–1409 BCE) signed a treaty with the Kassite king of Babylonia. He also rebuilt Aššur and recouped its advanced economic system. By the time King Eriba-Adad I was crowned in 1392 BCE, Assyria was exerting power over Mitanni.

King Eriba-Adad I's reign marked the beginning of the Middle Assyrian Empire (1392–1056 BCE). It was an era of comeback and recovery for Assyria, as it seized most of the Hittite territory and recovered northern Mesopotamia and the Levant. King Ashur-uballit I (1365–1330 BCE) crushed the Kingdom of Mitanni, which spurred the Hittites to join forces with Babylon against Assyria, but to no avail. King Ashur-uballit conquered Babylonia, installing a vassal king loyal to Assyria.

King Arik-den-ili (r. 1318–1307), whose name meant "long-lasting is the judgment of God," marched into northern Iran and pulverized the Gutians, who had wreaked havoc on central and southern Mesopotamia for centuries. He then turned his attention to the Levant, conquering Canaanite and Aramaean tribes. He instituted annual military campaigns and erected the great Ziggurat of Aššur.

Shalmaneser I (r. 1274–1245 BCE) subdued eight Anatolian kingdoms, overpowering a Mitanni and Hittite coalition. He supervised ambitious construction projects in Aššur and Nineveh and established Kalhu (the biblical Calah). His enterprising son, Tukulti-Ninurta (r. 1244–1207 BCE), took thousands of Hittite prisoners at the Battle of Nihriya. He demolished Babylon's walls and plundered the city's temples. He ruled Babylon for seven years as Babylon's first Assyrian king.

Tukulti-Ninurta authored an epic poem championing his victories over the Elamites. He triumphed over the Dilmun kingdom of Saudi Arabia and erected Assyria's new religious center and capital: Kar-Tukulti-Ninurta. Babylon reasserted independence after Tukulti-Ninurta's death, and internal unrest rocked Assyria. Then, Ashur-resh-ishi I (r. 1133–1116 BCE) rose as a forceful, victorious king who annexed the region of Iran's Zagros Mountains. He subdued the Amorites and Arameans and prevailed over Nebuchadnezzar I, subjugating Babylon once again.

The indomitable and renowned Tiglath-Pileser rose to power in 1115 BCE and ruled for forty-one years. He established Assyria as the Near East's leading power, striking terror as the world's premier military force. He overcame the Phrygians and Kaskians of Upper Mesopotamia and drove the Hittites from Assyria's Subartu province. He suppressed Malatia and Urartu (related to the Mitanni people) in eastern Turkey and the Armenian highlands.

Next, Tiglath-Pileser targeted Syria's Aramaeans, then blazed his way down the Mediterranean coast, seizing the Phoenician cities of Aradus (Arwad), Simyra (Sumer), Byblos, Berytus (Beirut), Sidon, and Tyre. An enthusiastic hunter of wild bulls, gazelles, lions, and elephants, he set sail into the Mediterranean, killing a *nahiru* (possibly a narwhal). He embarked on massive building projects and the restoration of ancient temples. His cuneiform tablet collections helped preserve the written history of Mesopotamia.

Within two decades of Tiglath-Pileser's death, a civil war ignited in Assyria between his son, Ashur-bel-Kala, and a usurper named Tukulti-Mer. Although the rebellion failed, it kept Assyria distracted, allowing a massive Hittite and Aramean invasion to take place. This caused the loss of Syria and Phoenicia.

Mesopotamia entered into its "dark ages" during the Bronze Age Collapse (1200–900 BCE) along with the rest of the Near East, North Africa, Greece, and the Balkan and Mediterranean regions. These three centuries saw massive upheavals and even the extinction of once-thriving civilizations because of the marauding Sea People, who devastated sea traffic and annihilated coastal cities from Egypt to Turkey. Since the ancient world was deeply interconnected through trade, its supply-chain breakdown was catastrophic, causing a widespread collapse.

Core samples taken from the Sea of Galilee in 2014 revealed a megadrought that lasted from 1250 to 1100 BCE. It would have killed off populations and encouraged mass migrations, perhaps even the mysterious Sea People. Israel was contending for Canaan's control against the Philistines, who may have been the Sea People who ravaged Greece and other eastern Mediterranean regions. Geophysicists discovered that a series of severe earthquakes rocked the Mediterranean from 1225 to 1175 BCE, which would have toppled cities and triggered tsunamis. This "perfect storm" of disasters plunged many civilizations into an abyss from which they could not recover.

Curiously, Assyria thrived through the first half of this era, as Tiglath-Pileser and other mighty leaders expanded the flourishing empire. However, the Hittite and Aramean invasions during Ashur-bel-Kala's reign began a century-long decline for Assyria. It led to the disastrous loss of territory, reducing the realm to the regions immediately next to Assyria. Nevertheless, Assyria's main domain in northern Mesopotamia persevered as a compact nation with a strong military and stable administration, while other countries were teetering on the brink of destruction. Greece, for instance, lost its written language and all its cities except Athens in these turbulent centuries.

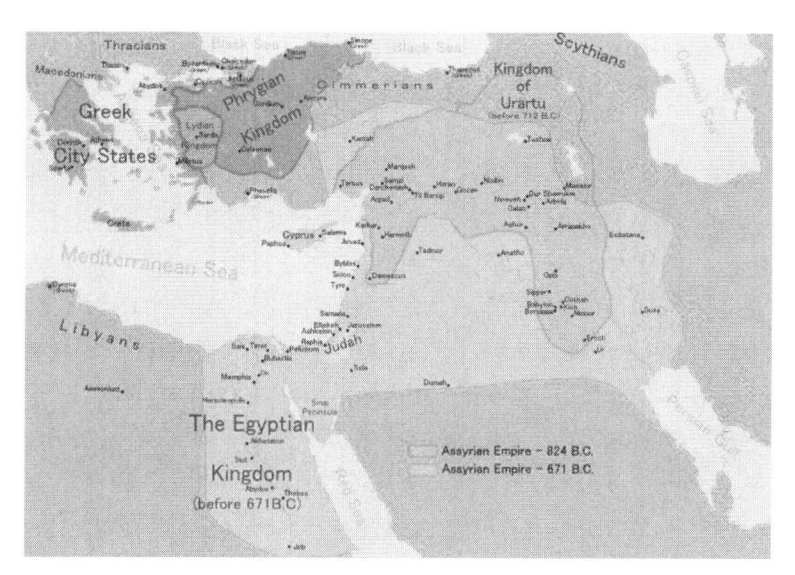

This map shows the extent of the Neo-Assyrian Empire.
Credit: Nigyou, CC BY-SA 3.0 https://creativecommons.org/licenses/by-sa/3.0 via Wikimedia Commons; https://commons.wikimedia.org/wiki/File:Neo-Assyrian_map_824-671_BC.png

Assyria recovered from the Bronze Age Collapse to enter its most prominent period: the Neo-Assyrian Empire, which lasted from 911 to 628 BCE. It grew exponentially, subjugating all of Mesopotamia, Egypt, the eastern Mediterranean coast, and part of Turkey. Shortly before the Bronze Age Collapse, the Assyrians began using iron weapons and war chariots. They developed lethal siege engines and engineer corps, making it the most technologically advanced military of the day.

Beginning with King Adad-Nirari II (r. 912-891 BCE), Assyria embarked on a massive expansion campaign. Along with its military technology, the Assyrians exercised brilliant battlefield tactics, using earthen ramps, mobile ladders, and siege towers on wheels to breach city walls. Meanwhile, combat engineers and miners dug tunnels under the walls to cause them to collapse. As the cities fended off the ladders and miners, the Assyrians used multiple battering rams to break down the gates and walls.

The Assyrians were a methodical, indomitable force. City by city and nation by nation, they gained territory in one campaign after another for over a century. Once they besieged a city, all hope was gone. However, after a little over a century, Assyria fell into a slump. Its rulers seemed to lack energy and ambition, their administration was disorganized, and their military was demoralized.

Finally, in 745 BCE, Tiglath-Pileser III ascended the throne, reorganized the bureaucracy, transformed the military into an efficient powerhouse, and retook the provinces that had broken away. He often relocated part or all of their population to prevent further uprisings. The Tanakh provides detailed insights into what it was like to be on the receiving end of the Assyrian war machine and part of its population-relocation program.

> "King Pul of Assyria [also known as Tiglath-Pileser] invaded the land and took the people of Reuben, Gad, and the half-tribe of Manasseh as captives. The Assyrians exiled them to Halah, Habor, Hara, and the Gozan River, where they remain to this day."
>
> Ketuvim, 1 Chronicles 5:26
>
> "During Pekah's reign, King Tiglath-pileser of Assyria attacked Israel again, and he captured the towns of Ijon, Abel-beth-maacah, Janoah, Kedesh, and Hazor. He also conquered the regions of Gilead, Galilee, and all of Naphtali, and he took the people to Assyria as captives."
>
> Nevi'im, 2 Kings 15:29

Shalmaneser V reigned next, from 727 to 722 BCE. He resettled part of the population of Babylon and other cities into Israel. A few years later, Sennacherib took the crown (r. 705-681 BCE) and honed Assyria's military the strongest it would ever be. He moved Assyria's capital to Nineveh, where he built a splendid palace with hanging gardens.

The Judean prophet Isaiah described what happened when Sennacherib sent his second-in-command from Lachish to Jerusalem, where he taunted King Hezekiah:

"Who are you counting on that you have rebelled against me? On Egypt? If you lean on Egypt, it will be like a reed that splinters beneath your weight and pierces your hand. Pharaoh, the king of Egypt, is completely unreliable!

I'll tell you what! Strike a bargain with my master, the king of Assyria. I will give you 2,000 horses if you can find that many men to ride on them! With your tiny army, how can you think of challenging even the weakest contingent of my master's troops?

When we put this city under siege, your people will be so hungry and thirsty that they will eat their own feces and drink their own urine."

Nevi'im, Isaiah

When King Hezekiah heard their report, he tore his clothes, put on sackcloth, and went into the temple. Soon afterward, King Sennacherib received word that King Tirhakah of Ethiopia was leading an army to fight him. Before leaving to meet the attack, he sent messengers back to Hezekiah in Jerusalem with this message: "Don't let your God, in whom you trust, deceive you with promises that Jerusalem will not be captured by the king of Assyria."

"That night the angel of the LORD went out to the Assyrian camp and killed 185,000 Assyrian soldiers. When the surviving Assyrians woke up the next morning, they found corpses everywhere. Then King Sennacherib of Assyria broke camp and returned to his own land. He went home to his capital of Nineveh and stayed there.

One day while he was worshiping in the temple of his god Nisroch, his sons Adrammelech and Sharezer killed him with their swords. They then escaped to the land of Ararat, and another son, Esarhaddon, became the next king of Assyria."

Nevi'im, Isaiah 36-37

The Greek historian Herodotus said millions of field mice had invaded the Assyrian camp, gnawing on bowstrings and destroying Assyrian arms. If so, perhaps the mice carried something like septicemic plague. Sennacherib was assassinated by two of his sons because he passed over the older son, Arda-Mulissu (Adrammelech), and instead made the younger Esarhaddon his crown prince. It did the young men no good to kill their father, as the Assyrians were horrified at the murder and did not support Arda-Mulissu's rule.

This bas-relief of Assyrian soldiers was found in Sennacherib's palace.

Credit: Gary Todd, CC0, via Wikimedia Commons;
https://commons.wikimedia.org/wiki/File:Ancient_Assyria_Bas-Relief_of_Armed_Soldiers,_Palace_of_King_Sennacherib_(704-689_BC)_(c).jpg

Esarhaddon and his son Ashurbanipal were ruthless yet efficient rulers. They continued to enlarge the empire's borders, stabilize the vast provinces, encourage the arts, and develop Assyria's legendary wealth. Yet, soon after Ashurbanipal's death, the Assyrian Empire began to crumble; it had grown too large to manage effectively. Taxes were exorbitant, power-plays and coups destabilized the monarchy, and revolts broke out in the provinces.

In 612 BCE, a coalition army of Persians, Babylonians, and Medes invaded and razed Nineveh, and most of the Assyrian ruling class fled to Harran in Turkey. Three years later, Pharaoh Necho II of Egypt marched toward Harran to lend his support to the remnants of the Assyrian leadership, but King Josiah refused to let him march through Judea. The Egyptians killed Josiah in the Battle of Megiddo, but the delay prevented Necho from reaching Harran in time. The Babylonians and Medes took the city. The fall of Harran spelled the end of the Assyrian state.

Chapter 6 – Daily Life in Assyria

What were the lives of Assyrians like 4,500 years ago when they built their first cities? How did their lives change over the next two millennia as their government and military developed? What new language did they begin using due to their vast population-relocation program? And what made the Assyrian religion and architecture distinctive?

We can glean the answers to many of our questions regarding daily life and culture in Assyria from the Library of Ashurbanipal. Around 600 BCE, the last Assyrian king, Ashurbanipal, formed the library with a clay tablet collection containing the literature of ancient Assyria, Sumer, and Babylonia. There were over thirty thousand tablets in his magnificent library, and they provide incredible insight into the Assyrian culture.

Assyria was a monarchy, and the Assyrians believed their god Ashur chose their king to be his earthly representative and high priest. The king served as Assyria's lead administrator, the army's commander-in-chief, and the "king of kings" over vassal nations. In Assyria's hereditary monarchy, the king designated one of his sons as his crown prince, usually the oldest, and appointed other sons as governors of nearby provinces.

The king had a court of chief ministers, including a chancellor to head the administrative staff. As with most Asian courts, many officials were eunuchs. A team of scribes managed the vast correspondence. In Assyria's earliest days, the king's rule encompassed several other city-states that made up the core Assyrian region in northern Mesopotamia. Then, as Assyria's military machine conquered other lands, some kingdoms became vassal states, while governors appointed by the king ruled others.

This painting depicts Ashurbanipal, "King of the world, King of Assyria."
Credit: Carole Raddato from FRANKFURT, Germany, CC BY-SA 2.0 https://creativecommons.org/licenses/by-sa/2.0 via Wikimedia Commons; https://commons.wikimedia.org/wiki/File:Exhibition_I_am_Ashurbanipal_king_of_the_world,_king_of_Assyria,_British_Museum_(45923437402).jpg

In the vassal kingdoms, the Assyrian emperor left the king of a conquered region in place as long as he submitted to Assyrian overlordship. If not, the Assyrian king would kill or imprison the rebel king and appoint a different king, generally from the defeated country's royal family. Most defeated nations continued as they had before, except they had to acknowledge the leadership of Assyria, pay tribute, and send troops to fight with Assyria's army. The tribute was a sort of tax; it was payable in money or goods.

Babylon was a neighbor and powerful rival of Assyria, so rather than make it a vassal kingdom, the Assyrian king himself, beginning with Tukulti-Ninurta (r. 1244-1207 BCE), ruled both Babylon and Assyria. Sometimes, the Assyrian king would appoint his brother or son to rule as a subordinate king.

Until the mid-8th century, the Assyrian Empire consisted of two zones: the conquered nations ruled by vassal kings and Assyria proper. When Tiglath-Pileser III became Assyria's king in 745 BCE, he reorganized Assyria's territorial administration, setting up smaller districts under the central government's control. He also initiated a third zone, which was most of Mesopotamia and Syria that fell under direct Assyrian control. Instead of vassal kings, the Assyrian king appointed provincial governors (usually Assyrian) and stationed a garrison of Assyrian troops in these provinces.

The Assyrians had a detailed law code that was much harsher than other Mesopotamian legal systems, such as Hammurabi's. Their style of imperialism was also despotic. Vassal kingdoms paid crushing tribute payments with nothing in return from Assyria other than "protection" by the Assyrian army, to which the vassal kingdoms had to contribute men. Many vassal kingdoms withered away, their people starving and impoverished, while Assyria reveled in unparalleled luxury.

In the 8th century, the Assyrians began the mass deportation of some especially rebellious conquered nations, as previously noted with Israel. The objective of the deportations was to disrupt the insubordinate strongholds. Sometimes, they deported the ruling class and left the ordinary people to tend the fields. Other times, they exiled the entire population to distant locations and brought the populations of other cities to the now-empty land. The exiles were usually not slaves; the Assyrians gave most of them the same rights as citizens, and some even rose to positions of preeminence in their new lands.

An estimated 4.5 million people were exiled to other parts of the Assyrian Empire, mostly Aramaic speakers. Aramaic became the lingua franca throughout the Assyrian Empire, both spoken and written. Aramaic had an alphabet that was much easier to learn than the cuneiform Sumerian and Akkadian scripts. Even most Assyrians started using Aramaic, although the ruling class continued to speak Akkadian and write in cuneiform. In 752 BCE, Aramaic joined Akkadian as the two official administrative languages.

The sensational Assyrian military developed one stunning innovation after another. They were among the first to fight with iron weapons and wear iron armor. In their Early Bronze Age days, elite warriors in chariots fought battles. With stronger and cheaper iron, Assyria could arm vast armies of foot soldiers who could march out to confront the enemy in terrifying numbers.

Cavalry forces gave the Assyrian military strength and agility in battle.
Credit: Osama Shukir Muhammed Amin FRCP(Glasg), CC BY-SA 4.0
https://creativecommons.org/licenses/by-sa/4.0 *via* Wikimedia Commons;
https://commons.wikimedia.org/wiki/File:Assyrian_horses.jpg

By the 15th century BCE, they had incorporated skilled cavalry riders. The Assyrians' interactions with the equestrian nomads of the Anatolian and Iranian highlands introduced them to cavalry techniques. These incredible horsemen rode without saddles or stirrups while shooting arrows, fighting with swords, or impaling the enemy with spears. They rode in pairs, with one soldier holding the reins of his mate's horse while the other used his weapons.

Until the mid-8th century BCE, the military was composed of young farmers and workers drafted for service. All able-bodied men were required to serve in the military. Usually, the younger men were the first to be called up, and they would train in camps before marching off on campaign. Men could also be summoned for construction projects or to farm the royal estates.

In the Neo-Assyrian Empire, the military continued drafting young Assyrian men each year, but they also had a professional army of highly-trained foreign troops who served for years. In the past, military campaigns took place during the "off" season when farmers weren't planting or harvesting their fields. More prolonged wars could be waged with a full-time military and permanent garrisons, which were set up throughout the empire.

The Assyrian military implemented brilliant, highly organized logistics to assemble the necessary supplies and food for campaigns, transporting them by camels. Soldiers packed inflatable bladders to use as flotation devices when crossing rivers. The innovative Assyrians were the first to use siege towers, battering rams, siege engines, and assault ladders, and the fearful apparatus and engineer corps traveled with the soldiers.

Even after developing a cavalry, the Assyrians continued using chariots. In Sumer, the earliest chariots were four-wheel or even six-wheel carts, but the Sumerians were already using two-wheel chariots before the dawn of the Assyrian civilization. Assyrian chariots had blades extending from the wheel hubs, which could sever the legs of any men or horses that got too close.

The Assyrians used psychological warfare, including terror tactics, to compel cities to surrender, such as capturing enemy soldiers, impaling them on long poles, and torturing them in view of the city walls. When the Assyrian army led by King Tukulti-Ninurta in 1225 BCE finally defeated Babylon, the desolation he wreaked on the city sent shockwaves throughout the region. The Assyrians flattened Babylon's walls, massacred or enslaved the citizens, pillaged the city, stole the sacred idol of Babylon's patron god Marduk (Bel), and stripped the Babylonian king naked, marching him in chains with his harem to Aššur. Tukulti-Ninurta boasted, "I filled the caves and ravines of the mountains with their corpses. Like grain piled beside their gates, I made heaps of their corpses."

Stealing Marduk was horrifically sacrilegious; it not only sparked horror in Assyria's enemies but also left the Assyrians aghast once the initial flush of victory abated. They feared Marduk was incensed at the Assyrians for destroying his city and stealing him from his temple! Crippled by the fear of Marduk's revenge, the Assyrians returned his idol to Babylon and rebuilt the city!

The long wars fought during the Middle Assyrian Empire established Assyria's reputation as a warrior nation. Their social stratification reflected the military's importance and the intrinsic contributions of the priests. The landed nobility farmed large estates and raised horses to supply the army. In its earliest history, Assyria, like other early city-states of Mesopotamia, had a self-supporting economy and grew enough food to sustain the population. There were also nearby resources for building reed or mud-brick houses.

Like other Mesopotamians, the Assyrians believed that each city was the home to its own patron god. Thus, the temple was the center of the city's spiritual and material life. The craftsmen, construction workers, weavers, and even the long-distance trade caravans were considered employees of the city's patron god. The king was simply a vice-regent for the god.

As time passed, the kings grew more powerful as secular rulers rather than simply being vice-regents and priests for the patron god. They began appropriating land and employed scribes and skilled craftsmen for themselves. Later, a private market emerged in the Assyrian cities that was unconnected to the king or the temple. This allowed the weavers, construction workers, and other workers to be self-supporting.

The Sumerians had used metal coinage since Ur's Third Dynasty (2112-2004 BCE); Ur-Nammu's law code mentioned fines of silver shekels. However, Assyria did not use metal currency until the Neo-Assyrian Empire under King Sennacherib (r. 705-681 BCE). Before that, Assyrians used seeds for currency, and law codes stipulated the seeds' value. The Assyrian temples served as banks. They kept written clay-tablet accounts of loans from merchants, landowners, and the temple itself. If the borrower repaid the loan by the due date, he did not have to pay interest, but delinquent payments incurred 20 to 30 percent interest!

Three social groups comprised Assyrian society: free citizens, serfs of the large estates, and enslaved people. Soldiers from conquered countries were incorporated into the Assyrian military. The craftsmen, scribes, and other highly skilled artisans became free Assyrian citizens and employed their trade in their new cities. Most farmers became serfs or tenant farmers on the Assyrian landed estates. Some captives, like Babylon's king and his family, became slaves. Assyrians could also sell themselves or their children into slavery to pay a debt. Even enslaved people had rights under Assyria's laws.

As Assyrian history progressed, women's social status decreased. For instance, older law codes stipulated that the family assets were to be equally divided if a couple divorced. However, a 14th-century Assyrian legal code stated that a man could divorce his wife without owing a financial payment to her. Men could beat their wives and pull out their hair with no penalty. A woman convicted of adultery could receive a sentence of a beating or death. A man could rape a woman (or another man) without punishment if the victim were a cult prostitute or of lower social status. If a man raped a virgin, she became his wife, but if he already had a wife, his wife was given to the virgin's father to rape.

While most ancient Mesopotamian civilizations buried their dead outside the city or cremated them, the Assyrians preferred to keep their departed loved ones at home. Wealthy Assyrians built a tomb for their deceased family members right in the house, while the common citizens dug a hole under their house to bury their dead. They would keep an oil lamp burning at the tomb or grave to signify that their deceased family member was with them.

Art and sculpture advanced swiftly as the Assyrians expanded their empire since they learned new techniques and styles from other civilizations. Assyrian artists reached stunning heights in their production of beguiling artwork. Archaeologists have unearthed captivating treasure troves of intricately worked jewels from the royal tombs of Nimrud and Nineveh. The Assyrian artisans created alluring items of gold, ivory, alabaster, and precious stones.

This bas-relief (circa 640 BCE) depicts King Ashurbanipal impaling a lion.
Credit: Osama Shukir Muhammed Amin FRCP(Glasg), CC BY-SA 4.0
https://creativecommons.org/licenses/by-sa/4.0 via Wikimedia Commons;
https://commons.wikimedia.org/wiki/File:Assyrian_king_Ashurbanipal_on_his_horse_thrusting_a_spear_onto_a_lion%E2%80%99s_head._Alabaster_bas-relief_from_Nineveh,_dating_back_to_645-635_BCE_and_is_currently_housed_in_the_British_Museum,_London.jpg

Assyrian sculptures and friezes followed Mesopotamian styles but on a grander scale; they were much larger than previous carvings. Rather than carving statues, the Assyrians preferred friezes and bas-reliefs: two-dimensional sculptures usually worked into a wall. Assyrian friezes were realistic and depicted fluid motion with exquisite detail. Many Assyrian friezes and bas-reliefs decorated palaces, celebrating the king's power in hunting and warfare.

What did the Assyrians wear? When they were pastoral sheepherders in their earliest days, they wore wool clothing. Early Mesopotamians domesticated flax to weave linen cloth, which would have been cooler for Assyria's hot summers. However, these clothes probably were worn mostly by the wealthy upper classes and priests. Sennacherib introduced cotton from the Indus Valley in the 8th century BCE.

Assyrian bas-reliefs and friezes typically show men wearing a knee-length or ankle-length tunic (the longer tunics denoted a higher rank). However, laborers are depicted wearing wrap-around skirts. Some of the tunics had angular hems: knee-length in the front and ankle-length in the back. In rare cases, men are depicted in the nude. Tunics were elaborately decorated with fringe and embroidery and dyed in bright colors.

Assyrian women wore brightly-colored ankle-length gowns, elaborate necklaces, earrings, headdresses, and fringed shawls. Men wore long capes over one shoulder, similar to Roman togas. Both men and women wore sandals and had braided hair. Small children ran about naked or with a little loincloth.

The Assyrians followed a polytheistic religion similar to the Sumerians and Babylonians. They even had some of the same deities. Their chief god was Ashur. One of Noah's grandsons, through his son Shem, was named Ashur in the Torah. He may have been the Semitic Assyrians' ancestor and acquired god-status over time, which often happened in ancient civilizations. Other important deities were the goddess Ishtar (goddess of love, sex, and fertility), Sin (god of the moon), and Tiamat (goddess of chaos and the sea). Just as each city had a patron god, each home had a household god.

The Assyrians sincerely believed the gods communicated with mankind via signs and omens. They paid close attention to anything unusual about the sun, moon, or stars. They analyzed birds' flights and pigs' actions and investigated bird entrails. The king had an entourage of shamans, astrologists, and priests to advise him on the gods' will concerning crucial decisions.

As Assyria grew from a modest city-state into a vast empire, communication, transportation, and infrastructure became increasingly complex. The Assyrians developed a well-ordered communication system to keep abreast of affairs in faraway provinces, using fire signals and couriers on mule or horseback for longer distances. To ensure swift delivery of messages, they built wooden bridges over rivers, paved roads through mountain terrain, and maintained a network of roads that extended to all points of the empire called the "king's road." Using relay riders, the Assyrians achieved unprecedented speed in message delivery, which was unsurpassed until the introduction of the telegraph over two thousand years later.

The Assyrians used camels to transport goods across desert regions and donkeys and oxen in more accessible terrain. They used barges and boats on the Tigris and Euphrates Rivers, which flowed from the Taurus Mountains of Turkey through Assyria, Sumer, and out into the Persian Gulf. Ships on the Mediterranean, Persian Gulf, and the Arabian Sea transported goods from as far away as India, northern Africa, and Europe.

These two lamassu in King Sargon's palace in Dur-Sharrukin feature the body of a winged ox with the king's head. Notice the creature on the left has five feet!
Credit: Vania Teofilo, CC BY-SA 3.0 https://creativecommons.org/licenses/by-sa/3.0 via Wikimedia Commons; https://commons.wikimedia.org/wiki/File:Human-headed_Winged_Bulls_Gate_Khorsabad_-_Louvre_02a.jpg

The Assyrians followed the typical Mesopotamian architectural styles with one notable exception: the scale. They loved constructing colossal buildings, which were protected from evil spirits by a gigantic statue called a *lamassu* that featured the king's head on a mythical creature's body. Assyrian kings enjoyed building projects; if they felt like the noblemen of the capital city were getting too belligerent, they would build a new capital city and move there, leaving the testy nobles behind and building up a new aristocracy.

They built breathtaking palaces and temples and designed captivating gardens and parks, diverting rivers to irrigate them. Assyrian architecture encapsulated Assyrian culture. They freely assimilated new elements from other civilizations and innovated startling new ways of doing things.

Chapter 7 – Babylon: An Overview

Driven by a great drought, mysterious nomadic shepherds swept into central and southern Mesopotamia in the 3rd millennium BCE. The Amorites demolished the former power structures like Ur's Third Dynasty. They also usurped the rule of ancient city-states like Kish and Isin and established extraordinary cities, most notably Babylon, which would rule an empire one day. The Sumerians called them Amurru or Martu and considered them uncivilized nomads. An Akkadian cuneiform tablet (circa 2300 BCE) described them as a bitter adversary of Sumer.

In the Sumerian creation myth called *The Marriage of Martu*, an Amorite fell in love with a Sumerian maiden, and she with him. Her girlfriend demanded to know why she wanted to marry this man:

> "Now listen! Their hands are destructive, and they have monkey features! They eat what our god Nanna forbids and don't show reverence. They never stop roaming about! Their ideas are confused; they cause only disturbance.
>
> This Amorite! He is dressed in sheepskins: he lives in a tent, exposed to the wind and rain. He doesn't offer sacrifices or bend the knee. He lives in the mountains,

ignoring the places of the gods. He digs up truffles and is restless. He eats raw meat. He lives without a house, and when he dies, he will not be buried according to proper rituals. My girlfriend, why would you marry Martu?"

Who were the Amorites? What were their origins? They spoke a northwestern Semitic language that was related to the Canaanite language. The Torah (Genesis 10) identifies the Amorites as descendants of Noah's grandson Canaan, saying they were a Canaanite clan, along with the Hittites and the ancient Phoenicians of Sidon. The Amorite herders migrated into central and southern Mesopotamia from the west, probably Syria, in vast numbers around the time of the devastating drought of the 4.2-kiloyear BP aridification event. The Amorites had become so prolific in Mesopotamia that around 2055 BCE, King Shulgi of Ur built a remarkable 155-mile-long wall to keep the Amorites out of Sumer.

Manuscripts from Babylonian archives stated the city of Babylon was founded on the banks of the Euphrates River in 2286 BCE (during the Akkadian Empire period) by a man named Belus. Belus was later elevated to god-status (Bel or Marduk) and became the patron of Babylon, similar to how the man Ashur became the patron god of Aššur. Babylon existed as a small, unimportant town for about four centuries as the Akkadian Empire drew to a close and the Old Assyrian Empire rose to power. By the 1800s BCE, it was an administrative center and a vassal town to the city-state of Kassala.

The Amorite Sumu-Abum (Su-abu) became the first king of the First Dynasty of Babylon in the mid-1800s BCE. He declared independence from Kassala. Sumu-la-El, who ruled the city-state of Babylon from 1817 to 1781 BCE, extended its territory, defeating Kish and other nearby cities and erecting a series of fortifications around the expanded domain.

Babylon's famous King Hammurabi was a fierce warrior yet keen administrator.
Credit: Mbmrock, CC BY-SA 4.0 https://creativecommons.org/licenses/by-sa/4.0 via Wikimedia Commons;
https://commons.wikimedia.org/wiki/File:(Mesopotamia)_Hammurabi.jpg

Babylon continued as a modest city-state until its sixth Amorite king ascended the throne in the 1700s BCE: the illustrious Hammurabi, whose extraordinary reign and law code we will explore in Chapter 11. Hammurabi's ambitious construction projects elevated Babylon from an obscure town to a stunning city with an efficient, centralized government. He drove the Elamites out of southern Mesopotamia and annexed Sumer, including Isin, Kish, Ur, Uruk, and Eridu. Within a few years, Babylon metamorphosized into the awe-inspiring Babylonian Empire.

And that was just the beginning! The Babylonian Empire continued to grow. Hammurabi led his army east to invade Iran, subduing the Kassites, Lullubi, Gutians, and Elamites. He then turned west toward his Amorite ancestors of the Levant and conquered the Mari and Yamhad kingdoms in Syria and Jordan. That last move brought him into conflict with the Old Assyrian Empire, which had been exerting power over the Levant and central Mesopotamia. This led to decades of on-and-off wars until Hammurabi won, making Assyria a vassal kingdom to Babylon.

The Old Babylonian Empire rapidly fragmented following Hammurabi's death. In the southernmost marshlands of Sumer, Sealand declared independence and formed its own dynasty. Assyria's vice-regent Puzur-Sin broke Babylon's shackles, regaining Assyrian independence in 1740 BCE. By the 1600s, Babylonia's territory had shrunk back to what it was before Hammurabi's rule, although it still boasted its large and beautiful city for a few more years.

King Samsu-Ditana reigned as Babylon's last Amorite monarch. In the 1500s, King Muršili I of the Hittites raided and sacked Babylon, carrying off loot and captives. However, he was disinterested in ruling the city. Like the Assyrians did later, he stole the idol of Marduk, but unlike the Assyrians, he kept Marduk, leaving Babylon as a ruined, unoccupied city.

Twenty-five years after the Hittite's savage assault on Babylon, the Kassites took possession of the abandoned city. Who were the Kassites? Their origin is somewhat of a mystery. They spoke a language isolate, which means it was unrelated to other known languages, and they may have come from the Zagros Mountains of Iran. They first appeared in written history when they unsuccessfully attacked Babylon during the reign of Nebuchadnezzar's son, Samsu-iluna (r. 1749-1712 BCE), about 150 years before Babylon fell to the Hittites.

Whatever their origins, the Kassites quickly proved to be a sensational power in Mesopotamia, ruling Babylon for almost four hundred years. Their king, Agum-Kakrîme, trounced the Hittites, retrieved Marduk's idol, and installed it back in Babylon. He built the new capital city of Kar-Duniash and rebuilt the ancient city of Nippur, which had laid neglected and practically abandoned. Within sixty-five years, the Kassites conquered Sumer, including the Sealand dynasty, and expanded northeast into the Diyala River region (present-day Baghdad).

And then, gradually, the Kassite power declined. It was eclipsed by the Assyrians, Elamites, and Aramaeans. The Assyrians staged a comeback during the Middle Assyrian Empire, and King Ashur-uballit brought the Kassites to their knees, installing a vassal king in Babylon. The Assyrian king Tukulti-Ninurta flattened Babylon's walls in 1200 BCE, stole the idol of Marduk, and ruled Babylon himself for seven years.

Then the Elamites attacked and plundered Babylon, and they stole Marduk again! They also stole the renowned stele with King Hammurabi's law code and hauled it back to their capital of Susa. What's worse, they captured the last Kassite king, Enlil-nadin-ahi, and took him back to Susa, ending the Kassite rule in Babylon in the 12th century BCE.

The Sumerian Second Dynasty of Isin rose to replace the Kassites as Babylonia's rulers. Under their King Nebuchadnezzar I (r. 1126-1104 BCE), the Sumerian-Babylonians marched to Elam and stole back Marduk's statue. Following this loss, Elam faded into obscurity for over a century. However, Nebuchadnezzar I was subsequently defeated by the Assyrian king, Ashur-resh-ishi I.

During the Bronze Age Collapse, Assyrian King Tiglath-Pileser I (1115-1076 BCE) pummeled Babylon in war. He annexed a massive swathe of Babylonia's lands and made the Babylonian kings vassals to Assyria until 1050 BCE. A cataclysmic famine weakened Babylonia, permitting the Aramaeans to make inroads in 1026 BCE. The Aramaeans deposed their king and plunged Babylonia into anarchy for twenty years.

The Kassites had been rebuilding power in southern Mesopotamia, and the new Kassite state regained control of Babylon around 1003 BCE. However, the Elamites had also been restoring their strength, and they seized Babylon about two decades later, only to have it fall to the Aramaeans. Meanwhile, another northwestern Semitic nomadic people, the Chaldeans, migrated from the Levant, settling in Babylonia's southeastern region on the banks of the Euphrates.

As Assyria recovered from the Bronze Age Collapse, it expanded once again, integrating Babylonia into its empire in 911 BCE. The Babylonians tried to reclaim independence, but Shalmaneser V cruelly put down the revolt, resettling a sizable portion of Babylon's citizens to Israel. Sennacherib appointed his oldest son, Ashur-nadin-shumi, as Babylon's king in 700 BCE. But when Sennacherib sailed across the Persian Gulf to attack Elam, the Elamites in Mesopotamia invaded Babylon and captured (and presumably killed) Ashur-nadin-shumi in 694.

Sennacherib retaliated by destroying Babylon. He razed it to the ground and diverted the Euphrates to flood the ruins. "I utterly dissolved it with water and made it like inundated land." Sennacherib also stole the god Marduk once again, and he put the god on trial before Assyria's patron god Ashur. The *Marduk Ordeal Text* suggests that Marduk died and was resurrected. After his own sons murdered Sennacherib, his younger son Esarhaddon ruled both Assyria and Babylon. He restored Marduk to Babylon and rebuilt the city his father had decimated, endeavoring to establish harmony between the two nations.

The Neo-Babylonian Empire arose in 626 BCE to become the most powerful Middle Eastern state. It began with Nabopolassar. He was the first of a new dynasty that ruled for over a century. Taking advantage of Assyria's unraveling, which had been caused by internecine conflicts, Nabopolassar led Babylon's rebellion. He and the Chaldeans signed a treaty in 616 BCE with Cyaxares, King of

Media, which was located in northwestern Iran (he was also the great-grandfather of Cyrus the Great). A royal wedding between Babylonia's Crown Prince Nebuchadnezzar II and Cyaxares's daughter Princess Amytis sealed the deal.

The Scythians, who came from the far northern steppes and allied with Assyria, held the Medes under their yoke. Cyaxares invited the Scythian overlords to a banquet, where he got them drunk before murdering them, freeing Media from Scythian hegemony. The Scythians switched sides, joining the Medes and the Cimmerians from the Black Sea in a massive coalition against Assyria. On horseback, hordes of Scythians and Cimmerians bombarded Assyria's far-flung provinces: Anatolia, Israel, and Judah. They even ravaged Egypt's coast.

While Nabopolassar fought the Assyrians in central Mesopotamia, the Medes, Scythians, and Cimmerians attacked and sacked Assyria's cities in northern Mesopotamia. In 612 BCE, a stupendous coalition force of Babylonians, Chaldeans, Medes, Scythians, Cimmerians, Persians (from the Eurasian Steppe), and Sagartians (of Iran) all joined together against Assyria. They sacked Nineveh in 612 BCE, ground Assyria into dust, and transferred Mesopotamia's rule back to Babylon.

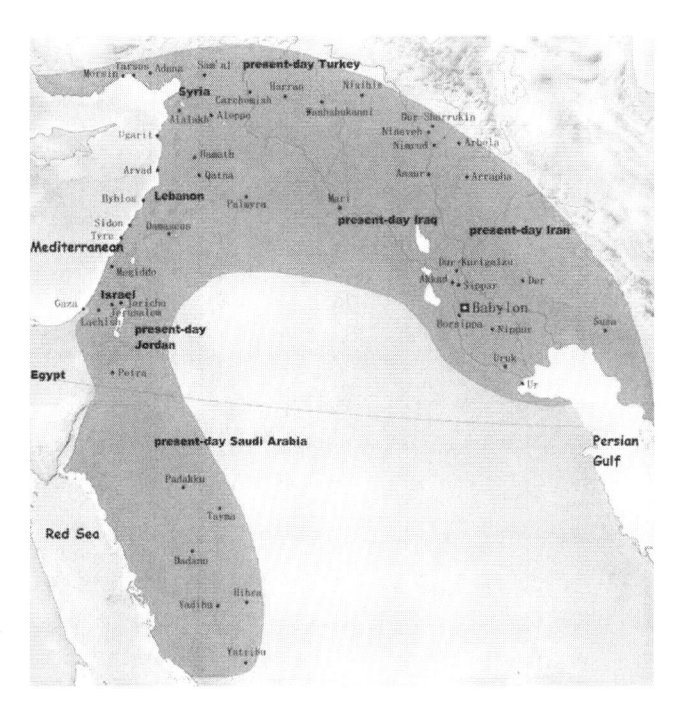

Neo-Babylonia's territory encompassed most of the Assyrian Empire's territory.

Credit: IchthyovenatorSémhur (base map) - Own work, CC BY-SA 4.0, Photo modified: zoomed-in, names of seas and present-day countries added; https://commons.wikimedia.org/w/index.php?curid=105149705

Nebuchadnezzar II ascended Babylon's throne in 605 BCE; by the end of his illustrious forty-three-year reign, he held sovereignty over all of Mesopotamia, eastern Iran, southern Turkey, Syria, Lebanon, Israel, Jordan, and western Saudi Arabia. In 597 BCE, Nebuchadnezzar marched on the rebellious Kingdom of Judah in the Levant and stripped the temple and palace of their gold and treasures. He also took King Jehoiachin prisoner, along with ten thousand captives, which included the royal family, military, craftsmen, and artisans.

Among the royal family were four youths: Daniel, Hananiah (Shadrack), Mishael (Meshach), and Azariah (Abednego), who Nebuchadnezzar trained, along with other young people from noble families, to enter his royal service. Daniel, a seer, remained as an advisor and dream interpreter to the Babylonian kings until 539

BCE when King Cyrus of Persia took Babylon. Daniel then briefly served the Persians.

When Judah rebelled again, Nebuchadnezzar laid siege against Jerusalem for two years while its people starved. King Zedekiah tried to escape one night, but the Babylonian troops overtook him, forcing him to watch as they slaughtered his sons. It was the last thing he would see, as the Babylonians gouged out his eyes and hauled him in chains to Babylon. After Nebuchadnezzar died in 562 BCE, his son, Amel-Marduk, released King Jehoiachin from the palace prison, where he'd languished for thirty-seven years. Jehoiachin dined at the king's table for the rest of his life. It is believed Zedekiah perished in Babylon.

Intrigue rocked the palace when Amel-Marduk's brother-in-law, Neriglissar, murdered him two years later, usurping the throne and reigning for six years. Another coup d'état brought Nabonidus to the throne, which he held for seventeen years. On October 12th, 539 BCE, Nabonidus's son and co-regent Belshazzar was at a grand feast with his nobles when he suddenly turned pale, his knees knocking, all strength drained from his body. A disembodied hand was writing on the palace wall! The aged seer Daniel was called in to inform Belshazzar that his days were numbered and that his kingdom would be given to the Medes and Persians. That night, after Cyrus the Great's engineers diverted the Euphrates River, his Persian forces entered Babylon without a struggle.

Babylon's government and political life evolved over time. In the earlier empire of the Amorites and Kassites, the kings micromanaged the government's trivial affairs. Their primary concerns, aside from warfare, centered on building temples, fortifications, and irrigation systems. The Babylonians, especially in the earlier empire, believed their kings were chosen by their patron god Marduk (Bel) and manifested the god's presence on Earth. In addition to their king, the Babylonians had an elected Assembly or Council of Elders. The Assembly was made up of wise men who offered counsel to the people and the king when they needed to make crucial decisions. Their main concern was not angering the gods.

The need for a consistent, established legal system impelled Hammurabi to write his legal code and involve himself in judging minor affairs. He embraced the Mesopotamian concept that the king was the guardian of justice. Hammurabi and other Babylonian kings had a systematic approach to assimilating new provinces they'd conquered; they would send specialists to organize and integrate new territories and coordinate population redistribution.

The Neo-Babylonian Empire exhibited increased interaction with foreign powers, an influential priesthood, and a constantly growing administrative system. Nevertheless, the Babylonians believed their ancient predecessors were nearer to the gods, and thus, they tended to emulate the old political structure. Some change was inevitable, but overall, the Babylonians were politically conservative. Marduk's priesthood grew dramatically in power during this era.

The Neo-Babylonian Empire initiated a cultural renaissance of art, exquisite sculptures, and outstanding architecture. The historian Herodotus spoke of Babylon as the most resplendent city of its time, with luxurious, breathtaking buildings and three rings of impenetrable walls, fifty feet tall and wide enough to host chariot races. The Ishtar Gate glistened with blue glazed tile mosaics depicting lions, dragons, and horses. Nebuchadnezzar's three palaces gleamed with yellow and blue glazed tiles. The god Marduk had finally returned to Babylon after the Hittites, the Assyrians, and the Elamites all stole his cult image, and Nebuchadnezzar ceremoniously enshrined him in the Esagila temple, which was just south of the great ziggurat in Babylon's center.

The reproduction of Babylon's Ishtar Gate is in the Pergamon Museum in Germany.
Credit: User:Hahaha, CC SA 1.0 <http://creativecommons.org/licenses/sa/1.0/>, via Wikimedia Commons;
https://commons.wikimedia.org/wiki/File:Pergamonmuseum_Ishtartor_05.jpg

According to the ancient Greeks, the Hanging Gardens of Babylon were one of the Seven Ancient Wonders of the World. They were supposedly built for Nebuchadnezzar's beloved wife, Amytis. The problem is that archaeologists haven't found evidence of these famous gardens. That doesn't necessarily mean they didn't exist, as new archaeological evidence is constantly unearthed, and much of ancient Babylon hasn't been excavated due to the high-water table. Some scholars think the Greeks meant Nineveh, which *did* have a well-documented garden built by Assyrian King Sennacherib. However, the Babylonian historian Berossus also documented the Babylonian Hanging Gardens, and numerous accounts give explicit details of how the Babylonians constructed the gardens. Despite the lack of archaeological evidence, literary evidence makes the Babylonian Hanging Gardens a near certainty.

From Babylon's inception, its people applied mathematics to observe daylight's length through the solar year. They recorded details of celestial phenomena, such as Venus's risings over twenty-one years, and cataloged constellations and stars in the Enuma Anu Enlil tablets. Medical texts date back to Babylon's First Dynasty, including the *Diagnostic Handbook* by Esagil-kin-apli around 1050 BCE, which described various illnesses, including their symptoms, prognosis, and recommended treatment.

In mathematics, Babylonians demonstrated an understanding of place value, square roots, the Pythagorean theorem (before Pythagoras), and how to measure the diameter and circumference of a circle. Technologically, they used a lever and pulley, a sundial, and a water clock and had a measurement system for long distances. They developed trigonometry and used mathematical models to study the earth's rotation.

Part of Babylonia's population, both men and women, knew how to read and write. Youths from the wealthier families attended school or were tutored at home. Merchants, engineers, and construction supervisors all had to keep records, and scribes recorded annals of government and translated ancient works from Sumer and elsewhere into the Akkadian language. They initially wrote in the cuneiform script, but once Babylonians began using the Aramaean alphabet in the Neo-Babylonian era, they translated masses of ancient literature: epic poems, hymns, and histories. Scholars had to be bilingual or trilingual and adept in both cuneiform and the ancient alphabet.

Babylonia was a civilization infamous for cruel and merciless slaughter on the battlefield, yet it was renowned for extending kindness and mercy to conquered people. The Babylonians could be guilty of impoverishing other cultures to enrich themselves, yet their proverbs taught morality, such as "smile at your enemy" and "treat evil-doers with kindness." They were a paradox, but they were a conglomeration of many cultures: Sumerian, Amorite, Kassite, Assyrian, Median, and more. They were complex, and because they assimilated culture and knowledge from multiple civilizations, the Babylonians reached great heights and left a lasting legacy on the Middle East and the world.

Chapter 8 – Babylon: Religion, Myth, and Creation

What were the religious beliefs of the Babylonians? What rituals did they practice, and what meaning did these rituals have? How important was religion to the Babylonians? This chapter will explore these questions and unpack the intriguing details of Babylonian religion. We will compare their creation myth to other Mesopotamian creation myths, investigate their pantheon of gods, and discover several other fascinating Babylonian myths.

Babylon shared many gods with Sumer and other Mesopotamian cultures, but the gods' positions and roles were somewhat different. Babylon's creation myth championed the victory of the younger gods over the older ones, just as the younger Babylonian civilization championed its victory over ancient Sumer.

In its infancy, when Babylon was just an obscure town, Marduk was its patron god, just as most other towns and cities in Mesopotamia had patron gods or goddesses. During Hammurabi's reign (r. 1792-1750 BCE), as Babylon rose from a city-state to an empire, Marduk rose to become Babylonia's national god. He surpassed Inanna (Ishtar) in popularity, and other female deities faded away since the Babylonians focused more on male gods. The

Kassites rose Marduk to even greater preeminence, making him the king of the gods.

The mušḫuššu was a dragon-like creature that represented Marduk.

Credit: Mary Harrsch from Springfield, Oregon, USA, CC BY 2.0 https://creativecommons.org/licenses/by/2.0 via Wikimedia Commons; https://commons.wikimedia.org/wiki/File:A_mu%C5%A1%E1%B8%ABu%C5%A1%C5%A1u,_the_sacred_animal_of_the_Mesopotamian_god_Marduk_on_the_Ishtar_Gate_of_Babylon_reconstructed_with_original_bricks_at_the_Pergamon_Museum_in_Berlin,_575_BCE_(32465090312).jpg)

It is thought that Babylonians had six hundred gods in their pantheon: three hundred heavenly gods and three hundred gods of the underworld. One of the gods was Anu (An), who was perhaps the most important god to the Sumerians. He was the god of the sky and the father of the gods. However, in the Babylonian creation myth *Enuma Elish*, Anu was one of the younger gods, although he was a leader and the grandfather of Marduk. The myth clarifies that Marduk is more powerful than Anu because Marduk overcame Tiamat when Anu could not resist her sorcery.

Nudimmud was the Babylonian name for the popular Sumerian Enki (Ea), god of fresh water. In Babylonian myths, he was Anu's son; he knew and excelled at everything. He put Apsu, the first of the gods, into a deep sleep and killed him, then lived on (or in) Apsu's body with his wife, Damkina, who gave birth to their son Marduk. In consultation with his son Marduk, Ea (Nudimmud, Enki) created humans to serve the gods.

Adad, another son of Anu, was the Babylonian storm god. His images show him carrying a lightning bolt or hammer with a bull's body or a dragon with a lion's head. Ishtar (Inanna), the sister of Adad and Enki, was the goddess of sexual love and war. In later Babylonia, Ishtar was connected to the planet Venus. She was the most popular goddess throughout Mesopotamia, and in Babylon, she was second only to Marduk in the pantheon.

Religious rituals connected humans to the gods. The humans were responsible for taking care of the gods' need for food and clothing, while the gods were the humans' source of justice, protection, and life itself. Babylon gods had dual characteristics of benevolence and violence. Rituals were intrinsic in keeping the gods happy and appeasing their anger. Religion was not optional; the Babylonians felt that keeping on the gods' good side was imperative for survival.

The Babylonians believed their everyday world overlapped with the spiritual dimension, which created anxiety and speculation. If they didn't keep the gods happy, they could be the victims of floods, famine, or invasion by other nations. Even in their mundane life, if they accidentally spilled or dropped something, they thought it was because of evil spirits. Thus, they often turned to sorcery to cast spells on their enemies or protect themselves from the dark forces. The earlier Babylonian kings and most Mesopotamian kings forbade sorcery, but in the Neo-Babylonian Empire, the kings had sorcerers and magicians in their retinue.

The state-sanctioned worship of Marduk, Ishtar, and the rest of the gods was an inherent part of Babylonian life. Temple priests, priestesses, exorcists, and other personnel dealt with worship and organized ceremonies. They dressed the gods and goddesses, served their meals, made sacrifices, recited prayers, and sang hymns. They exorcized evil spirits and purified the temple grounds and sanctuaries. Only certain people could enter the temple: the priests/priestesses, artisans and carpenters (who made the idols and built the temples), and staff who prepared the food offerings.

Care of the idols was a sacred duty because Babylonians believed their gods literally inhabited them. For instance, Adad, the storm god, lived within his temple idol but also floated around in the clouds, shooting out flashes of lightning and pouring rain down on the fields. Stealing or destroying an idol could incur that god's wrath; if enemies stole a city's patron god, the city would lose its divine protection. When Sennacherib attacked Babylon, Prince Marduk-apla-iddina II gathered up the city's idols and fled to the marshlands to protect them from being stolen or demolished by the Assyrians.

The New Year was the Babylonians' most important festival. The first month of the Babylonian calendar was Nisannu, which would fall in April or May in our Gregorian calendar. The New Year celebrations took place over several days. Reading the Babylonian creation myth *Enuma Elish* was an essential New Year ritual, along with taking Marduk's idol out of his temple and parading him through the streets. The people rejoiced and danced as they watched the idol travel to a small "vacation house." It would stay there for the festival's duration.

Babylonia's creation myth was the *Enuma Elish* or *The Seven Tablets of Creation*. It told the story of the god Marduk's victory over the older gods, how the world and humans were created, and how Marduk appointed the gods to their positions and duties. Multiple tablets containing the story have been found throughout central Mesopotamia, dating to around 1200 BCE, when Assyria conquered the older Babylonian empire. However, the colophons, or information about the tablets' publication written on the back of the tablets, stipulate that the newer tablets were copies or translations of older versions that dated to or before the First Babylonian Dynasty's establishment in the mid-18th century BCE.

The *Enuma Elish* includes many Sumerian gods, such as Anu (An) and Ea (Enki), who play leading roles in the story. However, the myth introduces a strictly Babylonian god, Marduk, as its main protagonist. Like the Sumerian *Eridu Genesis*, the oldest god is annoyed by the noise and clamor of the youngsters keeping him awake, except in the Sumerian version, it's the first humans who are noisy. In the *Enuma Elish*, it's the younger gods.

Enki was a popular god and a friend of mankind for all of Mesopotamia.
Public Domain; https://commons.wikimedia.org/wiki/File:Enki(Ea).jpg

In both stories, the older god decided to eradicate the irritating humans/younger gods, but the Sumerian version has Enki warning Ziusudra to build an ark to preserve human and animal life from the Great Flood. The Babylonian version descends into the macabre, as the younger gods save themselves by killing the older gods and creating the heavens, earth, and humans from their grisly remains.

The *Enuma Elish* story begins in the time before the heavens and the earth were created, with water churning in chaos. Only two beings existed: Apsu, the first, the progenitor, and his partner Tiamat, who gave birth to all. None of the other gods had been formed. Apsu and Tiamat mingled their waters together. Apsu's sweet water and Tiamat's chaotic, bitter ocean swirled together, creating the gods.

However, the young gods were extremely loud! Their clamor threw Tiamat into turmoil, jarring her nerves. Their dancing kept Apsu awake at night; however, he did nothing to quiet them. Tiamat was displeased with their behavior, but she kept silent; she didn't confront their tumultuous behavior. Finally, Apsu called his vizier Mummu, saying, "Let's discuss this with Tiamat!"

Apsu and Tiamat sat facing each other, discussing their noisy sons. "Their behavior is maddening! I can't rest day or night," Apsu raged. "I'm going to break up their way of life! I'm going to destroy them! Then, we can have peace and be able to sleep."

When Tiamat heard this, she fumed against Apsu's evil plot, raging, cursing, and wailing in grief. "How can we destroy what we've given birth to? Yes, their behavior is distressing, but let's extend grace. Let's tighten up our discipline and give them a chance to reform."

But Mummu the vizier spoke up. "My father, you should eradicate this lawless lifestyle so you can get some rest!"

Apsu's face beamed; he was pleased with Mummu, who backed up his plot to murder his sons. Mummu sat on Apsu's lap and put his arms around his neck, kissing him. Meanwhile, the younger gods heard about their father's plot and were frantic. Their knees buckled underneath them, and they collapsed, howling and moaning.

Enki decided to do something. He spoke an incantation over his father, pouring sleep over him until Apsu was in a deep slumber. Mummu wheezed in agitation, but Enki tied him up with a rope through his nose; he could do nothing to rescue Apsu now. Enki ripped off Apsu's crown and put it on his own head. He then tied Apsu up and killed him. He built his house in Apsu's body, holding on to Mummu's nose rope while doing so.

In his house, the Chamber of the Destinies, he sat with his wife, Damkina, in splendor. They conceived, and Damkina gave birth to Bel (Marduk), who had four eyes, four ears, and flames shooting forth from his mouth. His grandfather Anu created the four winds and gave them to Marduk, saying, "Let them whirl, son!"

Marduk created dust and drove it along with a hurricane. He sent a tidal wave crashing over Tiamat. Some gods chastised Tiamat; she had remained passive and did not interfere when the younger gods killed her partner. They insisted she must avenge Apsu. With the older god Qingu, her champion and new spouse, Tiamat called up the forces of chaos, creating eleven horrendous demons with sharp teeth and poison instead of blood. She sent them with weapons to slaughter her children.

Enki, who had killed Apsu and provoked the war, went to Tiamat to try to sedate her with magic spells and then trample her neck under his feet. But he couldn't resist her devious maneuvers; his incantations were unequal to hers. He fell silent at her fearful howls and slunk away. Then Anu went to Tiamat to appease her rage, but she was too terrible and struck fear into his heart.

None of the other gods wanted to confront Tiamat; they sat tight-lipped, staring at the ground. What were they to do? Then, the champion Marduk emerged, charging out in his chariot with its four steeds: the Trampler, the Destroyer, the Merciless, and the Fleet. He sent out the seven winds to harass Tiamat's entrails. When he saw Qingu's sorcery, he faltered at first, losing his nerve. But then he challenged Tiamat, angrily shouting, "You! Mother of the gods. Have you no pity for your children? Have you only contempt?"

Hearing these words, Tiamat lost all reason. Insane and trembling with rage, she spat out incantations and spells against Marduk, but he caught her in his net. As she shrieked loud, piercing cries, Marduk sent a hurricane into her gaping mouth, inflating her body. He then plunged a spear into her heart, tore open her entrails, and smashed her skull. He bound the eleven demons, trampling them under his feet, and bound Qingu.

Marduk then returned to Tiamat's corpse, resting as he surveyed her body. His father Enki had crafted a home out of Apsu's body, and Marduk would make a home from her body. He sliced her in two, like filleting a fish, and stretched out one half to make the sky while the other half became the earth. From her tears flowed the Tigris and Euphrates. Then he fixed the stars of the Zodiac in the sky to mark the twelve months and created Nanna, the moon, the god of the night. He appointed all the gods to their specific roles: three hundred in the heavens and three hundred in the underworld.

The other gods gathered around, cheering, kissing his feet, and giving kingship to Marduk. Marduk then consulted with his father Ea (Enki), and they decided to kill Qingu, "the one who instigated warfare." They created humans from his body. Ea created the first man, Lullu, from Qingu's blood to serve the gods, which freed the gods from mundane tasks and allowed them to better maintain order and keep chaos away.

The exhilarated gods proposed building Babylon as a home for the great gods and Marduk's resting place. They built Babylon's walls, constructed the temple of Esagil for Marduk, and created their own shrines. When they completed their building project, beer mugs were set out, and they all sat down to a festive banquet, toasting Marduk as king over the gods.

Curiously, the preeminent goddess Ishtar was not named in the *Enuma Elish*. However, she has several myths of her own, including her famous visit to the underworld. Ishtar's sister Ereshkigal was the queen of the underworld, and Ishtar's pretext for visiting the underworld was to mourn with her sister, whose husband had died. But the other gods suspected she was attempting a hostile takeover of the underworld.

Before making her descent, Ishtar carefully applied kohl around her eyes and draped herself in resplendent royal robes. She marched to the entrance of the underworld, banging on its gates, and ordered the gatekeeper to let her in. If he refused, she swore she would tear the gates off their hinges. He let her through the first gate but informed her she must remove a symbol of power as she passed through each gate. By the time she passed through the seventh gate, she was naked.

This "Queen of the Night" relief may depict Ishtar arriving naked in the underworld.
Credit: British Museum, CC0, via Wikimedia Commons;
https://commons.wikimedia.org/wiki/File:British_Museum_Queen_of_the_Night.jpg

Ishtar swiftly stole her sister's throne, but the seven judges of the underworld found her guilty of usurpation. They sentenced her to death and hung her body on a hook. Ishtar's death created pandemonium on earth, as Ishtar was the goddess of sexual love and fertility. Now, no one was making love and conceiving children. After Ishtar failed to return, her handmaiden Ninshubur went to the temples of the gods, pleading with them to rescue her mistress from the underworld.

Enlil, Nanna, and Anu refused to help, saying Ishtar brought her fate upon herself. But Enki realized that humans would die if Ishtar was not restored. He scraped the dirt under his fingernails and created two androgynous creatures to ask Queen Ereshkigal for Ishtar's body. They sprinkled Ishtar with the water of life, and she revived. But she couldn't leave the underworld unless someone took her place. From the underworld, Ishtar looked up to see her husband Tammuz (Dumuzi) *not* mourning her death! She picked him to replace her for half the year, and the demons would drag him to the underworld every year for six months.

Another Babylonian myth concerned Adapa, son of Enki, the first man to be created. Adapa was fishing when his boat overturned. In anger, he broke the South Wind's wings, and he had to go to heaven to apologize to Anu. Before he left for heaven, Enki warned him not to eat or drink anything while there, or he would die. Adapa apologized to Anu, who forgave him and offered him food and drink. Adapa refused the food, thinking it would kill him, but in reality, it would have made him immortal. He was tricked out of living forever.

A third myth was about Nergal, the god of war, who got into the underworld, slept with Ereshkigal, then tried to sneak away. She caught him and tried to kill him. He attempted to kill her, but they decided to get married and jumped back in bed! Before all this happened, Nergal was bored, so he decided to start a war. After all, the humans wouldn't respect the god of war if no fighting happened.

Nergal targeted Babylon for his war. Using sorcery, he tricked Marduk into leaving town for a while. The world descended into temporary chaos in Marduk's absence. However, Marduk returned from vacation before Nergal got his campaign off the ground. Nergal kept plotting, and eventually, Marduk left again. This time, Nergal plunged the world into horrible warfare and suffering and threatened to destroy the cosmic order. His vizier distracted him by starting a war on Mount Sharshar, which somehow quenched Nergal's rage. He came back to his senses, grateful that he hadn't destroyed the heavens and the earth. Marduk's absence in this myth may reference the times when the Hittites, Assyrians, and Elamites stole his statue.

Even when Babylon wasn't ruling much of the known world, it was still a place of religious pilgrimage, as it was considered a holy city. The Babylonians regarded their city as the center of the world, a sort of idyllic Eden, symbolizing cosmic harmony through Marduk's defeat of chaos.

PART THREE: Age of Innovation

Chapter 9 – The Epic of Gilgamesh

Over four thousand years old, the *Epic of Gilgamesh* may be the world's oldest written story. It is more than one thousand years older than Homer's *Iliad* and *Odyssey*. Partially written versions of the epic date to 2100 BCE, but its oral history undoubtedly traces back further. Tablet fragments with the story include Sumerian, Babylonian, and Akkadian gods, indicating that the epic originated in Sumer, with other Mesopotamian civilizations later adopting it. This chapter will unwrap the story itself and analyze its background and significance.

Archaeological and literary evidence places Gilgamesh as a real king in Uruk's history. As far as heroes go, Gilgamesh was a bit of an anomaly. He was two-thirds divine and one-third human, but his subjects were unhappy with their cruel, arrogant king. The most glaring reason was he felt entitled to rape the virgins in Uruk on their wedding night.

His subjects got a prostitute to partially tame a wild man named Enkidu, who possessed unnatural strength. They wanted him to challenge Gilgamesh and change the order of things. Instead, the two men hit it off and set off on adventures together. Enkidu's death forced Gilgamesh to recognize his mortality. And that's what made him a true hero; not his brilliant feats with grotesque monsters, or at least not *just* his brilliant feats, but acknowledging and accepting his humanity.

This stone carving from the Shara Temple depicts Gilgamesh wrestling two lions.
Credit: Osama Shukir Muhammed Amin FRCP(Glasg), CC BY-SA 4.0
https://creativecommons.org/licenses/by-sa/4.0 via Wikimedia Commons;
https://commons.wikimedia.org/wiki/File:Gilgamesh_in_a_Sculptured_Vase,_Shara_Temple,_Tell_Agrab,_Iraq.jpg

The *Sumerian King List* records Gilgamesh as the fourth king of Uruk. The *Sumerian King List* mentions Gilgamesh's father as "invisible" or supernatural, and the epic says his father was Uruk's second king, the "divine Lugalbanda." His mother was the goddess Rimat-Ninsun, so for Gilgamesh to be "one-third" human, his father must have been half-god. But that still doesn't work mathematically—maybe in myths, it doesn't matter.

The *Epic of Gilgamesh* has multiple ancient sources in several languages, and five Sumerian poems dating to 2100 BCE contain portions of the story. The oldest version of the entire epic is the Old Babylonian Tablets, which date to 1800 BCE; however, some tablets are missing or damaged. The Akkadian scholar-priest Sînlēqi-unninni compiled the best-preserved version between 1300 to 1000 BCE in twelve tablets, which were uncovered in Nineveh's Library of Ashurbanipal.

The themes in the *Epic of Gilgamesh* are enlightening in regard to Mesopotamian culture. They take us beyond grand inscriptions and bas-reliefs to the story of a flawed king, who was also strikingly handsome and unassailably strong. Although most of the story is a fantastical myth, it reflects real-life struggles. We gain insight into the people's frustration with their political leader, the depths of friendship between two men, and beliefs about death and immortality.

The *Epic of Gilgamesh* opens with a description of Gilgamesh, who crossed the ocean, explored the world, and sought eternal life. "He brought information of the time before the Flood. He went on a distant journey, pushing himself to exhaustion, but then was brought to peace."

Gilgamesh was the most beautiful and perfect of men. But he had a dark side, and the people of Uruk implored the gods for justice for the brides he had raped. So, the gods created a man who was Gilgamesh's equal in strength: Enkidu, the hairy man of the forest! He ate grass with the gazelles and jostled with the wild animals at the watering hole. One day, a trapper saw him at the watering hole and went rigid with fear. His heart pounded, and his face drained of color. He told his father of the wild man who had been destroying his traps and setting the wild animals free. His father told him to go to Uruk and get Shamhat, the prostitute; she would tame this mighty man.

So, the trapper brought Shamhat to the watering hole. When Enkidu saw her voluptuousness, he groaned with lust, and for seven days, he had intercourse with her. But afterward, the gazelles darted off when they saw him, and the wild animals distanced themselves. Shamhat asked him, "Enkidu, why do you gallop around with these wild beasts? Come to Uruk with me and meet Gilgamesh, who struts his power like a wild bull."

This terracotta wall panel from Ur, circa 2027-1763, depicts Enkidu.

(Credit: Osama Shukir Muhammed Amin FRCP(Glasg), CC BY-SA 4.0 https://creativecommons.org/licenses/by-sa/4.0 via Wikimedia Commons; https://commons.wikimedia.org/wiki/File:Enkidu,_Gilgamesh%27s_friend._From_Ur,_Iraq._2 027-1763_BCE._Iraq_Museum.jpg

Enkidu agreed to accompany Shamhat to Uruk to challenge Gilgamesh and change the order of things. Meanwhile, Gilgamesh dreamed that a meteorite fell from the sky and landed next to him. His goddess mother told him the meteorite represented the most rugged man in the land who would be his comrade.

On their way to Uruk, Shamhat took Enkidu to some shepherds, who put food and beer in front of him. Shamhat showed him how to eat human food. Enkidu drank seven mugs of beer until his face glowed, and he sang with joy! Then he bathed, rubbed oil on himself, and became human.

One shepherd told Enkidu of Gilgamesh's dastardly habit of raping the brides before their husbands could make love to them. This enraged Enkidu, and he stormed to Uruk, where a wedding had just taken place. He blocked the door to the bridal chamber, keeping Gilgamesh out. The two fought fiercely. The doorposts trembled, and the walls shook. After they wore each other out fighting, they kissed and became friends.

Forgetting the bride, they started talking about the ferocious monster Humbaba, the guardian of the cedars of Lebanon. With their joint strength, they determined to kill Humbaba. Hand in hand, they went to the forge to have weapons made. The Uruk elders counseled Gilgamesh not to be too foolhardy and told Enkidu to protect him. They then went to Gilgamesh's goddess mother, Ninsun, asking her to intercede with the sun god Shamash on their behalf.

The two men strode off, walking fifty leagues a day until they reached Lebanon. That night, Gilgamesh had a frightening dream that a mountain had fallen on him. Enkidu interpreted the dream to mean the mountain represented Humbaba, the monster, and that they would capture and kill him. For the next three nights, Gilgamesh had disturbing nightmares: a wild bull, a bolt of lightning, a tall, fearful creature. Each time, Enkidu assured him the dreams meant they would triumph over Humbaba.

On the fifth night, Gilgamesh had another disturbing dream. Tears were streaming down his face, but before he told the dream to Enkidu, the sun god Shamash warned them it was time to fight Humbaba. "Hurry! Don't let him enter the forest and hide in the thickets. He's only wearing one coat of armor, not all seven!"

Gilgamesh and Enkidu lunged at the Humbaba monster. Humbaba scoffed at them. "An idiot and a moron! Enkidu, you son of a fish! You don't even know your own father! I saw you when you were young but didn't bother you. Now you've brought Gilgamesh, an enemy! A stranger! I will feed your flesh to the screeching vultures!"

Just then, the ground shook, and they whirled around to see Mount Hermon split open. The clouds suddenly darkened, and the sun god Shamash sent thirteen winds against Humbaba. Locked in place by the winds, the monster begged Gilgamesh for his life. "Let me go! I'll be your servant! I'll cut down trees for you."

Enkidu warned Gilgamesh, "Don't listen to Humbaba!"

Humbaba turned to Enkidu. "You know the rules of the forest. I should have killed you when you were young. But I spared you! Now, clemency is up to you. Speak to Gilgamesh to spare my life!"

But Enkidu urged Gilgamesh on. "Kill Humbaba! Grind him up! Pulverize him!"

Gilgamesh killed Humbaba, and they cut off his head. They made a raft and sailed home. Enkidu steered while Gilgamesh held Humbaba's head. Before arriving in Uruk, Gilgamesh bathed, washed his hair, and cleaned his weapons. He shook out his long locks of hair, put on clean regal garments, tied his sash, and put his crown on his head.

His beauty captivated Princess Ishtar (Inanna, the patron goddess of Uruk). "Gilgamesh! Come, be my husband! You will have a chariot of lapis lazuli and gold harnessed to storming mountain mules! Kings, lords, and princes will bow before you and bring you tribute."

But Gilgamesh snorted. "What about all your previous bridegrooms? Where is your little shepherd Tammuz; you send him to the underworld for six months every year!"

One by one, he listed Ishtar's husbands, who had suffered terribly at her hands. Enraged, Ishtar flew to heaven to see her father, Anu. "Father! Gilgamesh has insulted me over and over!"

Anu replied, "What's the matter? Did you provoke King Gilgamesh?"

But Ishtar screeched, "Give me the Bull of Heaven so he can kill Gilgamesh! If you don't, I'll knock down the gates of the underworld, and the dead will come up to eat the living!"

Anu warned Ishtar, "If I give you the Bull of Heaven, Uruk will have seven years of famine. Have you stored enough food for your people?"

Ishtar nodded. "I have stored seven years of grain for the people and grass for the animals."

Anu handed Ishtar the nose rope of the Bull of Heaven. She led it down to Uruk. Once there, he snorted, and a pit opened up. One hundred men fell in. The bull snorted again. Another hole opened up, and two hundred men fell in. The third time he snorted, Enkidu fell in, up to his waist, but he jumped out and grabbed the bull by his horns. The massive bull snorted, lifted his tail, and flung out his dung behind him. Enkidu called to Gilgamesh, "I'll hold his tail, and you thrust your sword between his horns!"

Together, they killed the Bull of Heaven, ripped out his heart, and offered it to Shamash, the sun god. From the top of Uruk's wall, Ishtar hurled curses at Gilgamesh, but Enkidu wrenched off the bull's hindquarter and flung it at her. Enkidu and Gilgamesh washed their hands in the Euphrates and strode through Uruk, hand in hand.

Gilgamesh slays the Bull of Heaven in this Mesopotamian terracotta relief, circa 2255 BCE.

https://en.wikipedia.org/wiki/File:O.1054_color.jpg

But the gods were holding a conference in heaven, and Anu decreed that because Gilgamesh and Enkidu had killed the Bull of Heaven and slew Humbaba, one of them must die.

Enlil snorted, "Let Enkidu die, not Gilgamesh!"

But Shamash, the sun god, replied, "Wasn't it at my command that they killed Humbaba and the Bull of Heaven? Should innocent Enkidu die?"

Enlil angrily retorted, "You're responsible! You enabled them!"

The verdict fell on Enkidu, and as he lay dying, Gilgamesh's tears flowed like rivers. "Oh, my dear brother, why are they absolving me instead of you?"

Enkidu turned to Gilgamesh and told him about the horrible dream he had. It involved a gruesome demon overpowering him and dragging him down to the House of Darkness on the road of no return. "Remember me and all we went through!"

As the day dawned, Gilgamesh promised Enkidu all the creatures would mourn him: the gazelles, the four wild asses who raised him on their milk, the herds who taught him where to graze. The people would mourn him: the elders of Uruk, the shepherds, and the harlot. Even the land would mourn him; the pasturelands would shriek like a mother who had lost her child. Gilgamesh touched his friend's heart, but it beat no longer. "And I mourn you in anguish. You were my sword and my shield. What is this sleep that has seized you?"

Gilgamesh cried bitterly over his friend; deep sadness penetrated his core. He mourned over Enkidu for six days and seven nights. Gilgamesh would not allow his friend to be buried until a maggot fell out of his nose.

He then considered his own mortality, realizing that, like Enkidu, he, too, would die. He decided to travel to Utnapishtim for counsel. Who was Utnapishtim? He was the Noah-like figure from the Great Flood; the Sumerians called him Ziusudra in the *Eridu Genesis*. He was the man who built the ark and saved humanity and the animals. After all these years, Utnapishtim was still alive. Perhaps he held the key to immortality.

Gilgamesh traveled to Mount Mashu, the highest mountain in the sky, whose roots reach the netherworld. Scorpion beings guarded the gate. Although petrified with fear, Gilgamesh pulled himself together and approached them. The male scorpion-being called out to Gilgamesh, "Why have you traveled such a long journey?"

Gilgamesh answered, "I have come to see my ancestor, Utnapishtim, who was given eternal life. I must ask him about death and life!"

The scorpion-being said, "No mortal man has ever crossed through the mountain; for twelve leagues, it is dense darkness."

Gilgamesh convinced the scorpion-being to allow him through. After passing through the twelve leagues of horrifying darkness, Gilgamesh finally came to a beautiful land by the sea with cedars, agates, and fruit like lapis lazuli, carnelian, rubies, and emeralds. He sailed across the sea to the Waters of Death until he finally arrived in Utnapishtim's land.

Utnapishtim asked Gilgamesh why he looked so haggard and emaciated. Gilgamesh told him, "Should I not have such deep sadness within me? My friend Enkidu has died. Together we destroyed Humbaba and killed the Bull of Heaven. Now the fate of mankind has overtaken him. How can I be silent? How can I be still? Am I not like him? Will I lie down, never to get up again? How have you found eternal life?"

Utnapishtim replied, "I will reveal a secret of the gods. When the father god Anu decided to flood the earth, the clever god Ea came to my reed house and spoke through the wall, saying, 'Build a boat! Make all living things go inside.' So, I built the boat and coated it with bitumen. Then it started raining, submerging the mountains in water, overwhelming the people. The storm and flood flattened the land for six days and seven nights.

Then the rain stopped, and the wind calmed. I opened a vent, and fresh air came in. I fell to my knees, weeping. The boat lodged on Mount Nimush. On the seventh day, I released a dove; it flew around but couldn't find a perch, so it returned. I sent out a swallow, but it returned. Then I sent out a raven, and it did not return. So, I sent the animals out in all directions and sacrificed a sheep. The god Enlil told my wife and me to kneel, and he proclaimed us immortal."

As Utnapishtim spoke, the exhausted Gilgamesh struggled to keep his eyes open. "Wait!" Utnapishtim exclaimed. You've got to stay awake six days and seven nights!"

Apparently, staying awake was a key to immortality. But by that time, Gilgamesh was so deeply asleep that he did not awaken for days. Kindly, Utnapishtim gave him a second chance. He told Gilgamesh about a plant growing under the sea with thorns like a rose that would provide him with immortality. Gilgamesh attached stones to his feet and sank to the bottom of the sea. He found the plant, cut it, then cut off the rocks tied to his feet, and rose to the surface.

Unfortunately, as Gilgamesh traveled home with the plant of immortality, he stopped by a cool spring to bathe. A snake came along and carried off the plant, leaving its sloughed-off skin behind. Gilgamesh sat down weeping, tears streaming down his face. He returned home to Uruk, realizing the city was his destiny. Although his mortal body would die, he would live on through the city's people.

Gilgamesh achieved astounding successes but also dismal failures. He was courageous or at least had a daring disrespect for what would terrify most people. But his brazen overconfidence ended up getting his best friend killed. Gilgamesh's epic portrayed his attempt to escape his mortal constraints, answer inexplicable questions, and conquer mortality. But despite his extraordinary strength, he still had limitations. He was not omniscient, and one day, he would die just as his friend Enkidu died. Once he came to grips with these truths, he was genuinely heroic.

Realizing and accepting his true identity empowered Gilgamesh to live a wise and virtuous life. Well, at least virtuous in contrast to his former dishonorable ways; he most likely was not a stellar role model. But in whatever time he had left, he strived to grow and learn from his mistakes and be a better king. Perhaps he could even be an admired king, not for his extraordinary adventures but for what he could do for his kingdom.

Chapter 10 – Innovations and Inventions

Many technologies, scientific advances, and items we use every day without even thinking about originated in Mesopotamia. After all, it was the land of many firsts! Ancient Mesopotamia gave birth to a plethora of ingenious inventions and brilliant developments. Let's examine how the various Mesopotamian civilizations came to invent and use things like the wheel, the chariot, cuneiform writing, maps, mathematics, and even medicine.

Did you know that the first wheels weren't used for transportation? Archaeologists believe that a slow hand-turned pottery wheel called a tournette came first. An excavation at Tepe Pardis in Iran uncovered a tournette dating between 5200 and 4700 BCE. The fast, freely spinning pottery wheels with an axle emerged in Mesopotamia later; archaeologists found one in Ur dating to 3100 BCE.

The Sumerians invented the transportation wheel in the 4th century BCE. They inserted rotating axles into disks made from horizontal slices of tree trunks. The first wheels were solid pieces of wood; after about a thousand years, they developed a hollow wheel with spokes. This was much faster and lighter! Once the

Mesopotamians developed the transportation wheel, they surged ahead in utilizing carts for hauling big loads and chariots for fast transportation or battle.

Onagers draw this early wheeled cart in the "Battle Standard of Ur" (circa 2600 BCE).

https://commons.wikimedia.org/wiki/File:Ur_chariot.jpg

Once the wheel was invented, carts were used, pushed, or pulled by people or animals. Of course, this meant the people had to domesticate animals and train them to do things like pulling a cart. The first animals they used were oxen, donkeys, and a larger ass called an onager (which are almost extinct today). Mesopotamia did not have horses until the Akkadian Empire, and they were probably imported from the northern steppes. They had to figure out the technology of attaching the animals to the cart with a harness, breeching straps, collar, and pole.

Once the Sumerians succeeded in basic cart technology, they quickly developed chariots. Four-wheeled war chariots with solid wood wheels pulled by onagers are depicted in the Standard of Ur, dating to 2600 BCE. They were definitely meant for warfare, as some of the pictures show them running over the bodies of fallen warriors. They would have been slower and less maneuverable than spoked two-wheeled chariots, which Mesopotamians began using around the 2nd millennium BCE.

Horses were domesticated in Turkey's Caucasus region in the late 4th century BCE, but Mesopotamians didn't start using them until around 2400 BCE. Using horses to pull spoke-wheeled chariots brought about unprecedented speed. Around 1700 BCE, the Hittites developed an even faster chariot using wheels with only four spokes instead of six or eight. The Hittite chariot carried three men: the charioteer, the archer, and the shield-bearer.

Located between the Tigris and the Euphrates, with the Persian Gulf at its southern borders, water transportation in Mesopotamia offered an excellent opportunity for trade. Fish was an important food source, and boats made fishing more productive. Boats predated wheeled vehicles and provided another vital means of transportation in Mesopotamia. Southern Sumer's topography changed since river silting caused the Persian Gulf to shrink, but it once lay on the Persian Gulf's shores, near the Euphrates.

The Ubaid culture of the ancient coastal cities of Sumer invented the world's first sailboats, or at least the first for which we have physical evidence. Archaeologists uncovered several clay models of sailboats in Eridu, Mashnaqa, Oueili, Uruk, and Uqair, dating to the earlier Ubaid period (6250–4000 BCE). The sailboats facilitated long-distance trade on the Tigris and Euphrates Rivers and even 280 miles down the Persian Gulf coast to places like Bahrain, Qatar, and Saudi Arabia. Archaeologists have discovered Ubaid-period pottery in coastal settlements of the Persian Gulf.

The earliest sailboat had an uncomplicated design with a hull made initially from bundled reeds roped together and water-proofed by a thick layer of bitumen. Later, they used wood planks. They made square sails from linen, wool, or papyrus. The early sailors didn't have a way to control the sails' direction. The boaters had to wait until the wind was blowing in the direction they wanted to go. Although ancient Sumerian sailboats couldn't hold many people or much cargo, they were the prototype for future vessels that had a grander design and size.

The Sumerians developed the world's first writing system—cuneiform—early in their history. They needed a way to record business transactions, keep track of trade, and record events like astronomical anomalies. The first cuneiform, developed at the end of the 4th millennium BCE, used pictogram symbols representing words and objects. For instance, the word for fish looked like a simple drawing of a fish.

Thousands of tablets using these prototype pictograms and cuneiform still exist today, five thousand years later! They give us outstanding insight into the history and culture of ancient Mesopotamia. The first writers used the sharp end of a reed to draw in wet clay, which would then harden and preserve the writing. Pictogram writing was suitable for most nouns and some verbs, but it was difficult for more abstract words, like success, freedom, or good. Expressing past, present, and future tenses was also challenging.

The prototype pictograms evolved into cuneiform, which was easier to write. They still used wet clay tablets, but now, instead of drawing the word, they pushed the end of a cut reed into the clay to make wedge-shaped marks. The symbols were more stylized and abstract than the original pictures. Gradually, they began using symbols representing phonetics (sounds) for more abstract words.

Fortunately, for those who speak the English language, we only have to learn twenty-six letters of the alphabet. But one had to memorize over a thousand symbols to read and write in cuneiform; it took about twelve years for a scribe to be trained. The Mesopotamians reduced symbols to about six hundred by 2900 BCE to make writing easier. By comparison, if you learn the five hundred most basic Chinese characters, you can read about 75 percent of a newspaper in simplified Chinese. However, our modern language is more complex, as we have advanced technology and global concepts. The ancient Mesopotamians didn't require as many words.

About fifteen distinct languages, including Sumerian, Akkadian, Assyrian, Babylonian, Elamite, and Hittite, used cuneiform writing over a period of about three thousand years before the Aramaic and Phoenician alphabets gradually replaced it. In addition to clay tablets, the Mesopotamians carved cuneiform inscriptions into stone and began writing on parchment or papyrus.

	LINE CHARACTER. (Vertical)	LINE CHARACTER. (Rotated)	OLD BABYLONIAN.	ASSYRIAN.	NEW BABYLONIAN.
FISH					
REED					
DRINKING POT					
HOUSE					
RAIN					
CIRCLE, SUN					
KING (with his crown)					
MAN					
EAR OF WHEAT					
HEAD OF A MAN					
STAR					

TABLE ILLUSTRATING THE SIMPLIFICATION OF CUNEIFORM SIGNS.

This chart shows how cuneiform evolved from pictographs to abstract symbols.
https://commons.wikimedia.org/wiki/File:Evolution_of_cuneiform.jpg

The Babylonians innovated maps; the oldest that has survived dates to about 2300 BCE. Ancient Babylonian cartography used drawings on wet clay tablets, which reflect accurate surveying techniques. These ancient clay maps depicted hills and valleys and had labeled features; most maps were of small areas and used for city planning or hunting. More extensive maps were used for military campaigns and trading. The *Imago Mundi*, a Babylonian map of their world, dates to the 6th century BCE. It depicts Babylon on the Euphrates surrounded by Assyria, Armenia, and several cities. These locations are encompassed by the sea ("bitter river"). Eight outlying regions in triangular shapes form a star.

The ancient Mesopotamians had plenty of clay and mud available. They not only made clay bricks and wrote cuneiform in damp clay, but they also used it for their exquisite cylinder seals beginning in the 4th millennium BCE. They rolled these cylinders in soft clay to form impressions, which were often intricate pictures. Today, the ancient cylinders can be rolled in clay to obtain pristine examples of ancient Mesopotamian art. Scholars believe the Sumerians in Uruk invented the first cylinder seals around 3500 BCE, although they were used throughout the Near East.

People from royalty to commoners used cylinder seals when transacting business and sending mail. Made from marble, lapis lazuli, or metal, the owners wore them around their necks on leather lanyards or pinned to their clothing. Cylinder seals were like personal signatures that authenticated correspondence and important documents. Cylinder seals usually measure about three to four inches. Before developing cylinder seals, Mesopotamians used stamp seals, which measure less than one inch across.

A lapis lazuli cylinder seal circa 2800-2450 BCE is on the left. On the right is the impression the seal leaves on moist clay in this representation of the Myth of Etana.

https://commons.wikimedia.org/wiki/File:Sceau-cylindre_avec_la_repr%C3%A9sentation_du_mythe_d%27Etana.jpg

Many people say that math was not their favorite subject in school; nevertheless, we depend on math daily. Just think of how many times in the day we use basic counting, which was developed by the Sumerians. They used the twelve knuckles on one hand (not counting thumb joints) for counting by one, and each finger on the opposite hand represented twelve. So, they counted up to twelve on one hand and held up one finger on the other. They could do this up to sixty, using all five fingers (including the thumb).

We base our present-day counting on tens (ten, twenty, thirty, etc.), but Mesopotamians based their counting on sixty: the sexagesimal system (60, 120, 180, etc.) They divided the sky into 360 degrees and invented the 60-second minute and the 60-minute hour. Beginning in the 4th millennium BCE, Sumerians used objects to represent numbers: a tiny clay cone for the number one, a small ball for ten, a bigger cone for sixty. Gradually, they began using these objects to write numbers in cuneiform. Using the sexagesimal system, Sumerians started using an abacus prototype between 2700 and 2300 BCE.

The Babylonians developed the concept of zero. They were the first to use place values, with left-column digits representing larger values and right-column digits representing ones. Like the Sumerians, they used base sixty rather than ten. The number one in the left column represented sixty, so if you saw 2 / 7, it stood for (2 x 60) + 7 = 127.

The Sumerians quickly forged on from simple counting to advanced mathematics. By 3000 BCE, they began using basic measurements, and by 2600 BCE, they were using multiplication, division, square roots, cubic roots, and geometry. The Babylonians built on this knowledge. Beginning in 1800 BCE, they learned to use algebra and fractions; solve linear, quadratic, and cubic equations; and calculate reciprocal pairs, which multiply together to equal sixty. One Babylonian tablet, circa 1900-1680 BCE, calculated pi (π) to a value of 3.125.

The Plimpton 322 clay tablet, circa 1800 BCE, is a trigonometric table demonstrating that the Babylonians used sophisticated geometry and understood the Pythagorean theorem twelve centuries before Pythagoras was born. The tablet contains numbers in columns. Careful analysis of the numbers shows Pythagorean triples, where the longest side squared is equal to the sum of the squares of the two shorter sides.

One especially remarkable early Mesopotamian development was mathematical and scientific astronomy. The early Mesopotamians observed the movements of the celestial bodies—the sun, moon, planets, and stars—and reduced these observations to mathematical order. The Chaldeans in Mesopotamia probably initiated the study of astronomy in the 4th millennium BCE. Astronomy blended with religious elements, mainly astrology: the belief that the positions of the stars and planets affect people and events on Earth.

Through their study of the skies, the Chaldeans could accurately predict planets' motion, even apparent retrograde or backward motions (an illusion caused by Earth passing the outer planets in their orbits). They could also predict helical rising (when a star or planet becomes visible on the eastern horizon just before sunrise) and when planets or principal stars would come into alignment. The Chaldeans also calculated when the moon would go through its phases and when solar and lunar eclipses would occur.

The Babylonians began predicting eclipses in 721 BCE during the Neo-Babylonian Empire. Today, astronomers studying long-term variations in the lunar orbit consult the Chaldean and Babylonian eclipse records. The Babylonian months followed the lunar cycle, but the seasons followed the sun. So, they developed a lunisolar calendar of twelve months with four weeks of seven days. Every so often, they would throw in a thirteenth month to keep the calendar consistent with solar activity. An accurate calendar was intrinsic in an agricultural society, as it allowed farmers to plant and harvest at favorable times.

During the Neo-Babylonian Empire, Babylonians studied astronomy as a science disconnected from astrology. One contribution of Babylonian astronomers was dividing a circle into 360 degrees. They divided the day into twelve divisions; each division was a *kaspu*, the distance the sun travels in two hours (corresponding to thirty degrees). They split time into four-minute increments.

Over one thousand years before Hippocrates, medicine and doctoring were well-developed professions in Mesopotamia. Mesopotamians continued to refine their knowledge of pharmaceuticals and techniques in surgery and wound care through the coming centuries. Cuneiform tablets dating as far back as 3000 BCE document the evolution of medicine. Although Mesopotamian medicines involved religious rituals combined with physical treatments, doctors' facilities did exist independently of temples.

The Code of Hammurabi (1755–1750 BCE) had specific rules for doctors. Their fees had to be on a sliding scale depending on their patients' social class. The government could inspect a doctor's work, and doctors could be punished if they omitted necessary treatment or caused further harm to a patient. Although large-scale hospitals did not exist, physicians did have small clinics with beds for patients who needed round-the-clock care.

A Sumerian cuneiform tablet circa 3000 BCE lists fifteen medicines used to treat illnesses or for wound care, including potassium nitrate, cassia (cinnamon), myrtle, thyme, honey, and beer. They used all parts of plants—roots, seeds, bark, and sap—for wound care, laxatives, antiseptics, and to treat diseases. Doctors also treated pain using cannabis, mandrake, and opium. They used alcohol, myrrh, and honey as antiseptics. Inventory tablets in a Babylonian pharmacy, circa 1000 BCE, enumerated over 250 medicinal plants, 120 minerals, and 180 other medicines, which doctors mixed with alcohol, bouillon, honey, and oil.

Doctors performed surgeries in ancient Mesopotamia, including setting bones and excising wounds with bronze lancets. They castrated boys destined to become eunuchs. They used scalpels for surgeries, including cutting between the third and fourth ribs to relieve pleural effusion (fluid build-up in the membranes lining the lungs). They also operated on abscesses beneath the scalp, scraping away the affected bone.

The Mesopotamian shekel, which emerged over four thousand years ago, is the first known metal currency. In Semitic languages, the word shekel carried the idea of "weighing." The shekel was first documented about 2150 BCE during Naram-Sin's reign over the Akkadian Empire. In the Third Dynasty of Ur, Ur-Nammu's law code, written between 2048 and 2030 BCE, charged fines of shekels. These early shekels were not coins; they weren't round and flat with some sort of picture on them. They were simply a piece of metal (usually silver) that weighed about one-third of an ounce.

Many scholars believe the first stamped coins (flat and round with a picture on them) were minted in Lydia (in western Turkey) around 650 BCE. However, Neo-Assyrian King Sennacherib may have minted the first half-shekel coins decades before Lydia. One of his inscriptions mentions building a form of clay and pouring bronze into it to make half-shekel pieces. However, no one has yet found minted coins from Sennacherib's era.

Mesopotamians were also responsible for developing the first plow, called an ard, which a farmer would harness to an ox. The earliest "scratch plows," dating to around 5000 BCE, were wooden and heavy. The Assyrians began using iron plows around 2300 BCE. The plow's invention revolutionized civilization, enabling large-scale agriculture and allowing hunter-gatherer populations to remain in the same place. With a reliable food source, populations grew. People began building towns and cities, and they enhanced agriculture even more through irrigation.

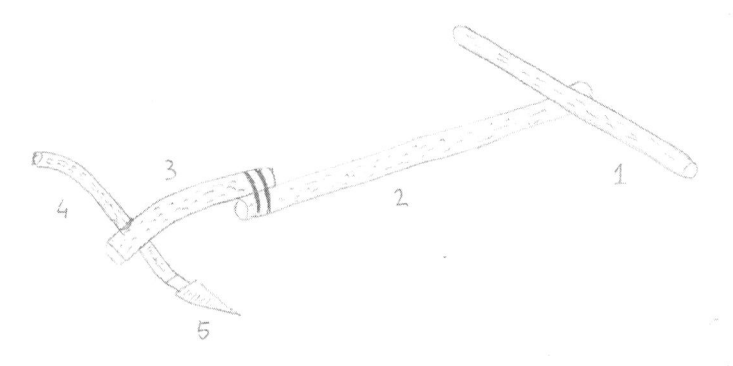

This drawing depicts a primitive ard: a type of ancient plow.
https://commons.wikimedia.org/wiki/File:AncientPlough.jpg

The Mesopotamians gifted us with many things that we consider basic necessities today. Their innovations and inventions have served the world for millennia. Their ingenious developments thousands of years ago intrigue and fascinate us, giving a glimpse of how people lived so long ago and what they did to organize and improve so many aspects of their lives. They must have constantly been brainstorming ways to do things more efficiently and effectively.

Chapter 11 – King Hammurabi and His Code

Among the numerous brilliant innovations birthed in Mesopotamia, written legal codes stand out for establishing law, order, and justice in society. King Hammurabi, who ruled Babylon from 1792 to 1750 BCE, was a sensational leader on many fronts. He was a relentless and ruthless conqueror and a canny administrator. But he is most remembered for his detailed legal codes that provided stability and unity for his expanding empire.

Hammurabi's stated goal in writing his law code was "to prevent the strong from oppressing the weak and to see that justice is done to widows and orphans, so that I should enlighten the land, to further the well-being of mankind." His legal treatise wasn't the first; the earliest known law code was Ur-Nammu's, which had been written three centuries earlier. The Assyrians also had a law code. But Hammurabi's was much more extensive; it had a total of 282 laws!

Who was Hammurabi? He was the sixth Amorite king in the First Babylonian Dynasty (1894-1595 BCE). The Amorites were nomadic shepherds, probably from Syria, who swept into Mesopotamia in massive hordes during the Bronze Age Collapse.

Hammurabi's predecessors established the modest city-state of Babylon in central Mesopotamia, not far from today's Baghdad. Babylon only consisted of a small town with surrounding agricultural lands in its early days. But Hammurabi's father, Sin-Muballit, had started consolidating several city-states under Babylonian hegemony.

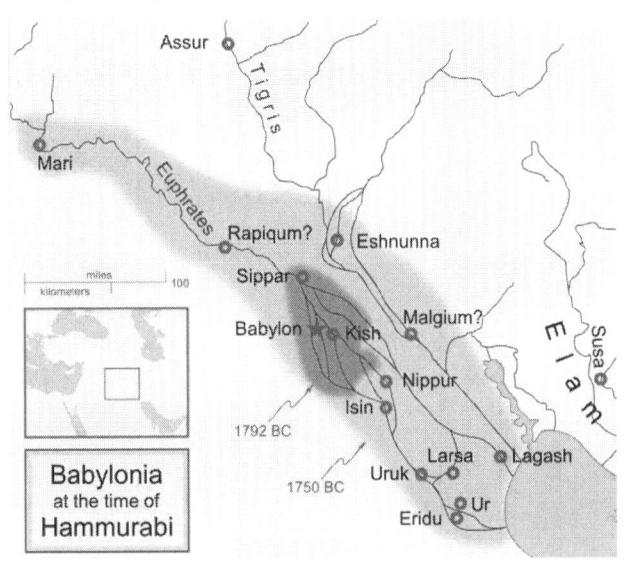

This map shows Babylon in relation to other central and southern Mesopotamian cities.

Credit: MapMaster, CC BY-SA 4.0 https://creativecommons.org/licenses/by-sa/4.0 via Wikimedia Commons; https://commons.wikimedia.org/wiki/File:Hammurabi%27s_Babylonia_1.svg

When Hammurabi was crowned king of Babylon, he had to contend with the complex politics of powerful rivals surrounding his minor kingdom. The Sumerian city-state of Eshnunna dominated the northern Tigris region. To the south, the Sumerian city-state of Larsa held supremacy over the Lower Euphrates. The Elamites in the east repeatedly invaded the small southern Mesopotamian city-states, exacting tribute. Although it was beginning to fragment, the formidable Old Assyrian Empire reigned in the north.

What did Hammurabi achieve as king of Babylon? Hammurabi took advantage of the relative peace in his early reign to focus on

Babylon's infrastructure. He dug canals to improve the irrigation system, built the city walls higher for more substantial protection, and built and restored temples, championing the worship of Babylon's ancestral god Marduk.

The power-hungry Elamites broke the region's tranquility by invading Mesopotamia's eastern plains and demolishing Eshnunna. The Elamites then attempted to instigate a war between Babylon and Larsa. Their objective was to conquer one or the other or both while the cities were distracted and weakened from fighting each other. However, the two cities didn't fall for the ploy. Instead, they allied and pulverized the Elamites.

The Babylonians were the ones who carried the victory. To Hammurabi's annoyance, Larsa didn't help much, leaving most of the fighting to the Babylonians. Once he settled affairs with Elam, Hammurabi punished his ally for failing to keep their end of the treaty. He annexed Larsa, which controlled most of southern Sumer. The fall of Elam and Larsa began Hammurabi's explosion of expansion, and most of Mesopotamia was brought under Babylon's sway by 1763 BCE.

Hammurabi proceeded to add Eshnunna and Mari to Babylonia's territory. After a protracted war with Assyria, he ousted King Ishme-Dagan I, making his son, Mut-Ashkur, a vassal king who paid tribute to Babylon. As Hammurabi grew his empire, he built Babylon up as a cultural and religious center: the premier "holy city" of Mesopotamia. Many civilizations coexisted in Mesopotamia, but Babylon's prominence as a cultural and spiritual center outlasted the Amorite dynasty.

This portrayal of Babylon shows how the city may have appeared.
https://en.wikipedia.org/wiki/Babylon#/media/File:The_walls_of_Babylon_and_the_temple_of_Bel.png

What was Hammurabi's significance in history? His quest to unify and promote peace in all his newly acquired city-states produced the legal treatise for which he is most famous: the Code of Hammurabi. Like the Code of Ur-Nammu, earlier law codes had given attention to compensating victims of crimes. Hammurabi focused on the corporal punishment of criminals and those who disenfranchised the poor and weak. Each crime had a specific penalty. These penalties are harsh by today's standards, but it is important to keep in mind that Hammurabi was actually limiting the harm inflicted when people took matters into their own hands. His law code was among the first to acknowledge the presumption of innocence.

What was Hammurabi's legacy? He was the most honored of the 2nd-millennium BCE Mesopotamian kings, and his subjects perceived him as an earthly representation of a god in his lifetime. After he died, the Babylonians and people from other civilizations revered him as a spectacular conqueror, admiring him for bringing peace, stability, and justice to Mesopotamia. The Babylonians championed his military campaigns as a sacred mission to "force evil into submission" and for spreading civilization and the worship of Babylon's patron god Marduk.

The paramount aspect of Hammurabi's legacy was his role as the consummate lawgiver for Babylon and all of Mesopotamia. Even after the Babylonian Empire faltered under his son, Samsu-iluna, not to mention that the Amorite dynasty completely collapsed 155 years after his death, the Mesopotamians continued to idolize Hammurabi as the paradigm for leadership and justice. When archaeologists discovered this remarkable king in the late 1800s, he rose to preeminence again for his contributions to the history of law.

The Code of Hammurabi contains 282 laws, which set standards for property legislation, trade and commerce, marriage and family, agriculture, employment wages, and regulation of slavery. It stipulated punishment for crimes such as false charges, false testimony, stealing, kidnapping, adultery, incest, and assault. It regulated the work of doctors, veterinarians, barbers, construction workers, and shipbuilders.

Hammurabi had his law code etched onto a black stone pillar that was over seven feet tall. The finger-shaped stele carved from durable diorite weighed four tons! Its surface held up well for four thousand years, but diorite is so hard that it must have been an arduous task to etch the cuneiform script. When archaeologists discovered this massive stele, it was over 250 miles from Babylon in Susa, the capital of the Elamites. How did it get there?

Jean-Jacques de Morgan, a mining engineer from France, headed up an expedition to Iran in 1901 to conduct archaeological excavations in Susa. That's when they dug up Hammurabi's black stele in three pieces. It must have been stolen in the mid-12th century BCE when the Elamites, under their king Shutruk-Nahhunte, raided and plundered Babylon. They took the stele back to Susa as booty, with Marduk's idol and the Kassite king Enlil-nadin-ahi.

The carving on the stele shows Hammurabi and Shamash.

Credit: Hammurabi, CC BY 3.0 https://creativecommons.org/licenses/by/3.0 via Wikimedia Commons; https://commons.wikimedia.org/w/index.php?curid=59794940

At the top of the towering stele was a two-and-a-half-foot tall relief carving of Hammurabi with Shamash, the Babylonian god of the sun, justice, and morality. One of the figures is standing, and the other is seated; opinions differ on who is who. The standing figure is probably Hammurabi, lifting his right arm in reverence to Shamash on his throne.

The bottom five feet of the finger-shaped stele have the 282 laws chiseled into the black stone with a cuneiform script. The text is interspersed with statements lauding Hammurabi as a devout and fair-minded king. The inscriptions don't explain the principles behind the laws; they seem to be based on legal precedent. The regulations provide several examples of "an eye for an eye" retribution; for instance, if a man puts out another man's eye, he must have his own eye gouged out. If he breaks another man's bone, his own bone must be broken. If a man knocks out the teeth of his equal, his teeth shall be knocked out in return.

Hammurabi wrote most of the laws in an "if-then" format. For instance, "If anyone steals the minor son of another, he shall be put to death." "If anyone finds runaway male or female slaves in the open country and brings them to their masters, the master of the slaves shall pay him two shekels of silver." "If he puts out the eye of a man's slave or breaks the bone of a man's slave, he shall pay one-half of the slave's value."

You'll notice from that last one that the standard of justice depended on whether the victim was someone higher in rank, a social equal, or an enslaved person. Sometimes the inequity was for the benefit of the slaves and freemen (landless citizens who usually did manual labor for others). For instance, Hammurabi set up a sliding scale for doctor's fees. If the doctor treated a severe wound, his fee would be ten silver shekels for a higher-class citizen, five for a freeman, and two for an enslaved person.

At the top of the stele is the carving of Hammurabi and Shamash. The law code etched into the stone covers the entire bottom of the monument.

Credit: Hammurabi, CC BY 3.0 https://creativecommons.org/licenses/by/3.0 via Wikimedia Commons; Photo modified: zoomed in; https://commons.wikimedia.org/w/index.php?curid=16931676

The same scheme applied to malpractice. If a doctor's treatment killed an upper-class citizen, the doctor's hands would be cut off. But if an enslaved person died under his care, he only needed to pay the owner for a new slave. The level of punishment also depended on the social status of the offender. Wealthy, high-ranking citizens only had to pay a fine if they injured commoners, not give up an eye or a tooth.

Although women's rights were closely tied to their fathers or husbands, they did have some protection. For instance, if a man accused a woman of adultery but could not prove it, his "brow shall be marked" (apparently a cut or tattoo). If a man raped a virgin betrothed to another man, he would be executed, and the woman would be blameless. If a man wanted to separate from his wife and mother of his children, he had to give back her dowry (money given by her family when they married) and give her the use of his fields and garden to support her children. When the children were grown, they and their mother would each get a financial portion. Then, the woman could "marry the man of her heart."

Hammurabi took false accusations and false testimonies quite seriously. For instance, if a man accused another of murder but couldn't prove it, the accuser must die. If someone falsely accused you of something, you could prove your innocence by jumping in the river. If you drowned, you were guilty, but if you escaped the waters, you were innocent. Your accuser would have to give his house to you.

Hammurabi held judges to a high standard as well. If a judge heard a case and charged someone a fine, but it was discovered later that the defendant was innocent, the judge would be deemed to have not done due diligence on the case. The judge would have to pay the defendant twelve times the fine he charged. The judge would also be publicly and permanently removed from the judge's bench.

Hammurabi felt the temples should be considered sacred. If anyone stole from the temple, they would be executed, and anyone receiving stolen goods from a temple would likewise die. Anyone dealing in stolen goods of any kind got the death sentence. For instance, what if your favorite earrings went missing, and you saw someone else wearing them, but they swore they honestly bought them from a merchant? Hammurabi said you should bring witnesses to the judge attesting the earrings were yours, and the person who bought the earrings would bring witnesses saying they had paid for them honestly. The merchant would die for being a thief if proven. You would get your earrings back, and the one who bought them would get their money back from the dead merchant's estate.

Hammurabi's laws about husbands divorcing their wives or taking a second wife were fairly strict. The husband had to provide financial support to a divorced wife in most cases. If his first wife became sick with an incurable disease or became disabled, he could not divorce her unless she wanted to leave him. In that case, he had to return her dowry. If she wanted to stay, he could take a second wife, but he had to continue caring for his first wife in his home for the rest of her life.

How was Hammurabi's law code significant? Well, first, let's see what Hammurabi had to say about the implications and relevance of his law code; it's etched on the stele with the laws:

> "I have guaranteed security to the inhabitants in their homes; a disturber was not permitted. In Babylon, I have the temple to speak justice in the land, settle all disputes, and heal all injuries. Let the oppressed, who has a case at law, come and stand before this my image as king of righteousness; let him read the inscription and understand my precious words: the inscription will explain his case to him; he will find out what is just, and his heart will be glad."

Did Hammurabi's law code influence the Law of Moses as some scholars contend? Let's consider the logistics. The Israelites lived one thousand miles away in Egypt during Hammurabi's reign, and, according to tradition, Moses wrote the Torah three hundred years after Hammurabi's death. As part of Egypt's royal family, Moses was trained in Egypt's legal system, although the Egyptians may have been aware of Hammurabi's law code. Moses did spend forty years living in Midian (today's Jordan and northwestern Saudi Arabia), but we don't know whether the Bedouins knew or followed Hammurabi's law code.

How similar is Hammurabi's code to the Torah's law? How are they different? They both have the law of restitution; they even mention injury to the eye, bone, and tooth almost word for word. "Anyone who injures their neighbor is to be injured in the same manner: fracture for fracture, eye for eye, tooth for tooth" (Torah, Leviticus 24:19).

In Hammurabi's law code, if a man could not pay a debt, he could sell himself, his wife, his son, or his daughter. They had to work for three years in the house of the man who bought them, and in the fourth year, they would be set free. In the Law of Moses, the same arrangement stood, except they would be set free in the Year of Jubilee, which came every seven years. Moses was adamant that Israelites were *not* to be treated as slaves; in this situation, their master should treat them as hired workers (Torah, Leviticus 25:39-43).

Some laws were similar yet different. For instance, what was the judgment if two men were fighting and one struck a pregnant woman? Hammurabi said that if the woman lost her unborn child, the man who hurt her had to pay ten shekels. But if she died, her assaulter's daughter would be killed. Moses said if the woman had a miscarriage, the man had to pay a fine; if the woman died, her assaulter, *not* his daughter, had to die. Moses was clear that everyone was responsible for their own sin. "Fathers shall not be put to death for their children, nor children for their fathers; each is to die for his own sin" (Torah, Deuteronomy 24:16).

Despite the striking similarities of several secular laws, many of the Torah's laws deal with sacred ceremonies, festivals, and regulations regarding God, such as "Don't worship idols" and "Don't worship any other gods." Hammurabi included nothing of this in his law code, but he had large sections regulating doctors, barbers, housebuilders, and shipbuilders that were not in the Law of Moses.

Interestingly, although Hammurabi said he wrote his laws to defend the orphans and widows, he had no rules expressly offering them protection. But the Torah certainly did, and it provided protection to aliens and the poor in multiple laws, such as, "Do not mistreat or oppress a foreigner, for you were foreigners in Egypt. Do not take advantage of the widow or the fatherless" (Torah, Exodus 22:21-22).

As we consider the historical significance of Hammurabi's laws, some are cringe-worthy by today's standards. Most of the punishments in the Code of Hammurabi were brutally harsh, such as cutting off someone's breast, ears, hands, or tongue. On the other hand, Hammurabi was a forerunner in promoting legal concepts like considering an accused person innocent until proven guilty. His laws recognized a defendant's intentions: was the crime willful or accidental? Today, most legal codes consider premeditation, the intent to cause harm, and mitigating circumstances. In this regard, Hammurabi's law code served as a prototype for modern laws.

Chapter 12 – Zoroastrianism

Zoroastrianism, one of the world's oldest religions still practiced today, emerged as Mesopotamia's primary religious school of thought during the Persian dynasties, beginning in the 5th century BCE. An especially notable aspect of Zoroastrianism was something approaching monotheism: the belief in one god. The other ancient Mesopotamians were polytheistic, except for the Jews. This means they worshiped many gods. Let's explore the origins of Zoroastrianism, their beliefs, and their core values.

Zoroastrianism's origins are somewhat obscure because no written documentation of this religion existed before 440 BCE. When the Greek historian Herodotus wrote about the Persians in general, he mentioned some customs that probably were Zoroastrian, although he didn't name them. He said they had no idols or temples but offered animal sacrifices to Zeus on the highest mountains. (He likely meant Ahura Mazda when he said Zeus.) He said they also offered sacrifices to the sun, moon, earth, fire, water, and winds. Herodotus said they worshiped the god they called Mithra. (Mithra was a Vedic god who became a Zoroastrian *yazata*, a lesser deity). Herodotus mentioned "sky burials," which means they left corpses exposed after death, a Zoroastrian custom. Other Mesopotamian civilizations buried their dead.

The Zoroastrians passed down their religious heritage orally. They did not write it down until they produced a master copy of the Avesta (their original scripture) in the 5th century CE during the Sasanian Empire. They didn't record any founding dates, but most scholars believe the religion probably emerged between 1500 to 600 BCE in northeastern Iran. It then spread south and west, infiltrating Mesopotamia.

Some scholars believe the Gonur Depe archaeological site in Turkmenistan (which dates from 2400 to 1600 BCE) suggests an earlier existence of Zoroastrianism because archaeologists found temples with fire altars and a preparation area for the *soma* (*haoma*) drink that is part of Zoroastrian worship. But the Vedic religion, which gave birth to Zoroastrianism, existed in that region during that period; fire sacrifices and the intoxicating soma drink were intrinsic to Vedic worship as well.

In 550 BCE, Persia's Achaemenid Empire rose to dominance over the Middle East and beyond, and Zoroastrianism surged in popularity during this era. It quickly spread east to modern-day India, Pakistan, Afghanistan, Tajikistan, Kyrgyzstan, Uzbekistan, and Turkmenistan. It spread west around the Black Sea to Turkey, Macedonia, and Greece, down the Mediterranean to Syria, Lebanon, and Israel, and south to Egypt and Libya.

What were the other major religions of ancient Mesopotamia when Zoroastrianism emerged? Most ancient Mesopotamians were polytheistic, worshiping a similar pantheon of gods, which included Anu, Ea, Shamash, and Ishtar, with some local deities rising to prominence like Marduk and Ashur. Abraham of Ur abandoned his father Terah's polytheism to become the monotheistic patriarch of the Israelites around 2100 BCE. Moses established Judaism as a monotheistic religion at Mount Sinai in 1446 BCE.

Did Judaism influence Zoroastrianism or vice versa? Both religions share core theology but also have differences. For instance, the Jews practiced circumcision, and the Zoroastrians did not. The

Zoroastrians prayed to Azura Mazda and lesser deities like Anahita and Mithra. In contrast, Jews prayed only to YHWH (Jehovah) and believed angels were God's messengers but were not meant to be worshiped.

The Assyrians and Babylonians had exiled most of the Jewish population to Babylon or other places in Mesopotamia, beginning with Tiglath-Pileser III of Assyria in 733 BCE and ending with Nebuchadnezzar of Babylonia in 597 BCE. The Jews would have interacted with the Persian Zoroastrians even before Cyrus conquered Babylon and certainly after.

Who founded Zoroastrianism? Around 1500 to 1200 BCE, perhaps even more recently, a man named Zarathustra (later called Zoroaster by the Greeks) lived in the region bordering today's Iran and Afghanistan. He belonged to the Spitama clan: an Indo-Iranian nomadic herding tribe that practiced the polytheistic Vedic religion. The Vedic worshipers had no temples or idols but offered animal sacrifices to a sacred fire and consumed a mind-altering drink from the soma plant.

The Dakmeh (Tower of Silence) in Yazd, Iran, is where Zoroastrians left bodies for vultures to eat. They believed this prevented decaying bodies from polluting the soil.

Credit: Fars Media Corporation, CC BY 4.0 https://creativecommons.org/licenses/by/4.0 via Wikimedia Commons; https://commons.wikimedia.org/wiki/File:Zoroastrians%27_Dakhmeh_of_Yazd_201 90316_02.jpg

Zarathustra was a married Vedic priest with three sons and three daughters. While engaging in a Vedic purification rite at the age of thirty, he had a vision of a supreme being: Ahura Mazda ("Wise Lord"). After this epiphany, Zarathustra repudiated Vedic polytheism and began teaching his disciples to worship Ahura Mazda. He wrote hymns (the Gathas) to this god, helping the people to understand Ahura Mazda's nature. His followers called themselves Zartoshtis or Zoroastrians.

Some believe Cyrus the Great (Cyrus II), King of Persia, was a Zoroastrian. Zarathustra's teachings may have influenced him, but we have no evidence that Cyrus practiced Zoroastrianism, although it became popular under his reign. Cyrus never mentioned the god Ahura Mazda in any of his inscriptions. He did have an inscription legitimizing his rule that said the Babylonian god Marduk appointed him as king. The Ketuvim records that in his first year as king,

Cyrus sent a proclamation saying the God of heaven had appointed him to rebuild the Jewish temple at Jerusalem. Cyrus returned the items Nebuchadnezzar had looted from the Temple in Jerusalem to the Jewish exiles returning to Jerusalem (Ketuvim, Ezra 1).

At any rate, within several decades, Zoroastrianism became the de facto religion of the Achaemenid Empire. Darius I (r. 522-486 BCE) was the first Persian king known to worship Ahura Mazda. The Persian kings were highly tolerant of other religions and did not force conversions of conquered people. However, as the Persian Empire spread, Zoroastrianism spread with it.

What do Zoroastrians believe? They worship Ahura Mazda: the completely good, uncreated, universal god who created the world. However, they also worship the Amesha Spenta and *yazatas*. These beings are hard to explain; they are created yet immortal. They seem to be "divine sparks" or lesser divine entities. They are sometimes compared to the angels and archangels of Judeo-Christianity. However, the Zoroastrian priests invoke them by name in their hymns and prayers as if they were deities, and some Persian kings built temples to these lesser divinities.

Most of the seven Amesha Spentas and dozens of *yazatas* were gods and goddesses in the ancient Vedic religion or Iranian pantheon, and some are deities in today's Hinduism. During Artaxerxes II's' reign, he invoked the deities Mithra, god of the sun, and Anahita, goddess of water, alongside Ahura Mazda. He built temples and statues to Anahita in Babylon, Ecbatana, and Susa. The Sasanian dynasty repaired and maintained Anahita's temple in Istakhr.

It is not entirely accurate to define Zoroastrianism as a monotheistic religion, although it was closer to monotheism than the polytheistic pantheons of Mesopotamia and surrounding civilizations. Clearly, Ahura Mazda is the chief divinity who created these other deities, and Zoroastrianism teaches they are under him as emanations of his divine power.

Zoroastrianism is a dualistic religion, meaning the world has two competing forces. The first force is goodness and light, represented by the Amesha Spenta: the "Bountiful Immortals who are good rulers and possessing good sense." Goodness and light struggle against darkness and evil, represented by Ahriman, who is something like Satan. Goodness and evil both exist but separately and in opposition. The goal is to incapacitate Ahriman and the evil and darkness accompanying him. This dualism involves both cosmic forces of the universe and moral forces of the mind.

The dualism of cosmic forces encompasses the continuing antagonism between good and evil in the universe. While the good god Ahura Mazda is at war against the evil Ahriman (Angra Mainyu), they are not opposites in the sense of being equal, similar to how YHWH (Jehovah) of Judeo-Christian theology is not equal to Satan but above him. Angra Mainyu (Ahriman) is the toxic evil energy combating Ahura Mazda's perfect creative energy.

Cosmic dualism means day and night, good and evil, and life and death. Ahriman persistently attacks the pure and perfect world Ahura Mazda created, polluting it with sickness, death, drought, famine, and other calamities. The *daevas* (demons) assist in his evil quest as the adversary of all that is good and true. The *daevas* were ancient Vedic deities of war and violence that became evil spirits in Zoroastrianism.

Moral dualism goes on in a person's mind and spirit in the battle between good and evil. Zoroastrians believe in free will; each person chooses to either follow *Asha* (truth and righteousness) or *Drui* (deceit and evil). One's choice determines their destiny: misery in life and hell after death for those who choose Drui or peace in life and heaven for those who select Asha. A person's choices bring either joy or distress, truth or falsehoods, peace or anxiety. The choices one makes determine whether they are helping Ahura Mazda or Angra Mainyu.

All mankind must choose Asha over Drui to conquer evil and bring paradise to Earth. Zoroastrianism holds a firm belief in heaven and hell and a day of judgment. At the end of the world, everything will return to its pristine and perfect state. Even people who made the wrong choices in life, the damned ones, will, in the fullness of time, reunite with Ahura Mazda in heaven as he ultimately prevails over evil.

Zoroastrianism's core teachings include following the path of good thoughts, good words, and virtuous deeds. One does not practice goodness to earn any reward; rather, one should be good for the sake of goodness. Zoroastrianism teaches that practicing charity spreads happiness and aligns one's soul with Asha. Men and women are spiritually equal and share spiritual duties.

For some reason, the Zoroastrians apparently did not have written scriptures for hundreds of years. The religion arose in a nomadic tribe, so the people were perhaps more accustomed to singing and telling their traditions. But even when they assimilated into the literate Persian culture, they still didn't write down any scriptures, or at least any that were preserved. There may have been some scrolls that Alexander the Great destroyed when he burned down Persepolis (a religious center in Iran) around 330 BCE. It seems that the mobeds, the Zoroastrian priestly caste, memorized and transmitted their teachings orally for at least one thousand years until the late Sassanian Empire, around 550 CE.

This sacred flame in the Yazd temple in Iran has reportedly burned since 470 CE.
Credit: David Stanley from Nanaimo, Canada, CC BY 2.0
https://creativecommons.org/licenses/by/2.0 via Wikimedia Commons; Photo modified: zoomed in; https://commons.wikimedia.org/wiki/File:Sacred_Eternal_Flame_(8906006775).jpg

When the Zoroastrians finally wrote their scriptures down, they developed an alphabet expressly for their holy book. They used letters from Persia's old Pahlavi script, a descendent of the Aramaic alphabet, which, like Hebrew and Arabic, was read from right to left and contained only consonants. The Zoroastrians added in Greek vowel sounds.

The oldest Zoroastrian scripture is the Avesta, named after the ancient Iranian language Avestan. The oldest section of the Avesta is the Gathas, which means "a divine song, a song of praise, a sacred hymn." These were five metrical compositions of the Prophet Zarathustra to worship Ahura Mazda, the Amesha Spenta (or Spenta Mainyu, the seven created immortal gods or archangels), and the *yazatas* (lesser gods or angels). The priests sang these scriptures or chanted them from memory.

When they were finally written down, these five hymns filled seventeen chapters. The Gathas also included several sacred prayers used in the Zoroastrian worship liturgy, and they were considered the source of spiritual nourishment and protection for the soul. Zarathustra's disciples composed the rest of the Avesta, the core teachings. Then, priests memorized these scriptures, recited them in worship, and passed them down through the centuries.

The Khordeh Avesta (meaning the little, minor, or younger Avesta) is the second part of Zoroastrianism's sacred scriptures, and it is much longer than the first. It contains a confession of faith, commentaries, short readings on the earlier Avesta, prayers for various times of the day, and details for observing rituals. It's something like the Book of Common Prayer. These scriptures aren't nearly as ancient as the Avesta, and there isn't even a standard text; different publications vary concerning the contents. They were likely composed in the late Sassanian period or even later. The Khordeh Avesta was probably memorized along with the Avesta, although the "Zand" section on exegesis was more of a work in progress. It tended to be changed and lengthened.

The two most important symbols of Zoroastrianism are water and fire, which represent purity. Purification is an essential concept of Zoroastrian daily life and religious rituals. As part of the quest to overcome evil, they endeavor to keep their minds and bodies clean and clear and strive for a pristine environment. Fire represents the zenith of purity. Water is a living element protected by Anahita (the ancient Iranian goddess of water, fertility, wisdom, and healing who became a *yazata* in Zoroastrianism).

Zoroastrian ceremonies and rituals are always performed in the presence of sacred fire. They sometimes worship in "fire temples" or Agiaries, which have an altar with a continuously burning eternal flame. They believe that three of their ancient temples, the "great fires," came from Ahura Mazda when the world was created. The fires represent Ahura Mazda's light, which illuminates the mind; thus, the fires must burn perpetually.

Zoroastrians practice the prayer ritual of Yasna daily, which honors creation. It begins by drawing water from the Agiary for purification. The Yasna service is directed toward Anahita, displaying the reverence for water. Yasna also involves rituals of preparing the sacred beverage (soma or haoma), which they drink with a bread offering. Yasna is meant to maintain the cosmic integrity of Ahura Mazda's perfect creation.

The Yasna includes devotional texts from the Khordeh Avesta, which are recited by priests and lay members. Twenty-one hymns are chanted to the *yazatas* or lesser deities under Ahura Mazda. In the ceremony, the priests ask theoretical questions of Ahura Mazda, such as the creation of the world and who set the sun and stars on their paths. Each day of the month in the Zoroastrian calendar is devoted to a *yazata*, and a hymn is recited to the deity of the day. Various short prayers and blessings are also recited. Attending the Yasna service helps maintain good actions, thoughts, and words and ward off the forces of evil. Zoroastrians pray facing the fire or sun, which represents Ahura Mazda.

In ancient times, Zoroastrians practiced "sky burials" in their *dakhmas* or "towers of silence." These were tall, flat-topped structures where they placed dead bodies, which vultures would eat. In their minds, burying a dead person meant defiling the pristine earth with a decaying corpse. Once the bones were clean and bleached by the sun, the people gathered and placed them in ossuaries (lime pits). Today, the Parsi Zoroastrians of Mumbai, India, still practice this sky burial custom.

Sky burial is also practiced today by the Tibetan tantric Buddhists and was practiced by Mongolian Vajrayāna Buddhists before communist rule. The ancient Vedic religion that gave birth to Zoroastrianism also practiced sky burials. The Vedic religion shaped Hinduism and prescribed sky burials in the *Paingala Upanishad*, an Indian Vedic scripture, although feeding dead loved ones to vultures never really took off in India. But Hinduism gave birth to Buddhism, and the tantric-Vajrayāna division of Buddhism carried the practice of sky burials to Tibet and Mongolia.

The Faravahar became a Zoroastrian symbol in the Achaemenid Dynasty.

Permission is granted to copy, distribute and/or modify this document under the terms of the GNU Free Documentation License, Version 1.2 or any later version published by the Free Software Foundation; https://commons.wikimedia.org/wiki/File:Faravahar.png

An ancient symbol of Zoroastrianism is the Faravahar: a bearded man reaching one hand forward and holding a ring in the other. He stands or sits in front of a pair of wings outstretched from another circle. The symbol of the wings and wheel goes back to ancient Egypt, predating Zoroastrianism, but the wheel and wings with the man appeared in Zoroastrian art around 550 BCE. No one is quite sure what it symbolized in ancient times, but the circles may represent eternal life. Today, it is the national symbol of Iran.

As with most religions, festivals and holy days play a vital role in the Zoroastrian faith. Six festivals relate to the seasons and predate Zoroastrianism. Nowruz celebrates the New Year on the day of the spring equinox. Other festivals relate to the *yazatas*, the lesser gods or angels in Zoroastrianism who were Vedic deities, like Mithra, Anahita, Atar, Rashnu, Sraosha, and Verethraghna.

The Navjote or *Sedreh-Pushi* is an initiation ceremony that receives children into the Zoroastrian faith. This occurs sometime between their seventh to twelfth birthday. Each child receives their first kusti and sudreh (a sacred cord and shirt) and engages in the "kusti ritual," where they tie the kusti cord three times around the sudreh shirt. This ceremony represents the Zoroastrian ideals of "good words, good thoughts, and good actions" and is led by a priest called a *mobed*.

Whatever happened to Zoroastrianism? For about one thousand years, Zoroastrianism was the de facto religion of three Persian empires: the Achaemenid (550-330 BCE), Parthian (247 BCE-224 CE), and Sasanian (224-651 CE). The Muslim-Arab conquest of Persia defeated the Sasanian Empire in 651 CE and broke Zoroastrianism's dominant influence over the Middle East. The Islamic Arabs forced the Zoroastrians to pay extra taxes for continuing their religion.

Islam had a three-fold effect on Iranian Zoroastrians. Some converted to Islam, and others continued to practice Zoroastrianism in remote, rural areas; they still do in the desert communities of Yazd and Kerman in Iran. A mass exodus of Zoroastrians, especially the priests and their families, sailed over the Arabian Sea to Gujarat in western India between 785 to 936 CE. The Indians called them Parsis, and they were influential during the British rule over India.

How widespread is Zoroastrianism today? They continue as a religious minority of up to thirty thousand devotees in Iran. About 60,000 Parsi in India and 1,400 in Pakistan continue as

Zoroastrians. Worldwide Zoroastrian diaspora communities are especially prevalent in North America, Australia, and Britain, with up to 200,000 worshipers. Freddie Mercury, the lead singer of the rock band Queen, was of Parsi descent. He practiced Zoroastrianism and was buried with rites by a Zoroastrian priest.

Do you wonder if there's a connection between the god Ahura Mazda and the Japanese car? Yes, there is! It was a play on words. The pronunciation of the car company's founder Matsuda was similar to the god Mazda. But how would the Japanese know about Mazda? In Uzbekistan and Afghanistan, the worship of Buddha and Ahura Mazda syncretized in the 1st century CE; they had a Buddha-Mazda. Esoteric Buddhists took the worship of Buddha-Mazda, the god of light, to China and Japan, where it's still practiced. The Japanese were familiar with Mazda, the god of light, so the new company adopted Mazda's name as a "light" in the car industry.

PART FOUR: Here Come the Persians (550 BCE–330 BCE)

Chapter 13 – The Achaemenid Empire Rises

The spectacular Achaemenid Empire, founded in 550 BCE by Cyrus the Great, ranks as the world's first superpower; it had been the most extensive empire at this time. It brought three major global regions—Mesopotamia, India, and North Africa—under one central government. This cultural intermingling created a dynamic surge in science, technology, and culture that persisted for over two centuries before the empire fell to Alexander the Great in 330 BCE.

From Egypt and Libya to the south, the colossal empire stretched up and around the Mediterranean, west to northern Greece and Macedonia. It spread north, encircled most of the Black Sea, then east to the southern Caspian Sea, then northeast to present-day Kazakhstan, down to India, and back west along the Arabian Sea, around the Persian Gulf, and across the Arabian Peninsula.

Valuable knowledge about the awe-inspiring Persian Empire comes from several sources, including Herodotus's *Histories*. He was born into a Greek family in Anatolia around 484 BCE, when it was part of the Achaemenid Empire. His family participated in the Greek insurrection against Persia, so he wrote about the Greco-

Persian Wars from the opposition's perspective. He focused on the Persian court's immorality, extravagant luxury, and political intrigues.

In the Tanakh (Old Testament), we have insider information from two Jews within the Persian palace. The first was Daniel (Belteshazzar), one of three administrators for the satraps (Persian governors) under Cyrus the Great. The other was Nehemiah, cupbearer to King Artaxerxes I. Another valuable source is Xenophon, who was born around 430 BCE. He was a Greek who fought as a mercenary for the Persians and wrote *Cyropaedia*, a biography of Cyrus the Great.

The First Persian Empire is often called the Achaemenid Empire after Achaemenes: an obscure ancestor of some, if not all, of the kings of the First Persian Empire. The Persians were nomadic Indo-Iranian herders from the north and east of Iran who settled in southwestern Iran's Persis region by the 9th century BCE. The Assyrians dominated them initially and then Babylon, but the Persians allied with the Medes around 612 BCE to get out from under Babylonian hegemony.

Cyrus II created the largest empire yet seen in the ancient world.
Credit: Arya.Go, CC BY-SA 4.0 https://creativecommons.org/licenses/by-sa/4.0 via Wikimedia Commons; hhttps://commons.wikimedia.org/wiki/File:Cyrus_the_Great_II.jpg

Xenophon recorded that Cyrus II (Cyrus the Great) was the son of King Cambyses of Anshan (Persia) and the grandson of King Astyages of Media, his mother's father. His parent's marriage represented the alliance of the Medes and Persians against Babylonian control; however, the Medes originally held overlordship. Cyrus married his beloved Cassandane, who was also of the Achaemenid dynasty, and became king of Persia in 559 BCE upon his father's death. He took the throne name Cyrus II after his paternal grandfather, Cyrus I; his birth name was Agradates.

The Babylonian Nabonidus Chronicle records that his grandfather King Astyages attacked the Persian kingdom because his grandson Cyrus refused to submit to Median overlordship. However, Astyages's army and some nobility defected to Cyrus during the three-year struggle. Finally, Cyrus captured his grandfather, but he spared his life. The Medes and Persians renewed their alliance, but the Persians now held overlordship.

Although Herodotus said that Cyrus became king of both the Medes and Persians after the war with his grandfather, the historian Xenophon recorded in *Cyropaedia* that Astyages's son, Cyaxares II, became king of the Medes at this point. Perhaps both accounts are correct; Cyaxares was likely a vassal king under his nephew Cyrus. Inscriptions on the Harran Stele, depictions on the Persepolis reliefs, and the Greek Aeschylus's *The Persians* support Xenophon on this.

Xenophon said that after conquering Babylon, Cyrus gave his uncle Cyaxares, King of Media, a palace in Babylon. Cyaxares II gave his daughter to Cyrus in marriage (Cyrus's first wife Cassandane had died shortly before Babylon fell, according to the Nabonidus Chronicle). Some scholars believe that Cyaxares II's throne name was Darius and that he was the Darius the Mede who Daniel said conquered Babylon at the age of sixty-two and then briefly administered Babylon (Ketuvim: Daniel 5-6).

Cyrus is mentioned twenty-three times in the Tanakh (Old Testament). Isaiah, a prophet in Jerusalem when the Assyrian king Sennacherib besieged it, wrote this prophecy about Cyrus 150 years before Cyrus ascended Persia's throne:

> "This is what the LORD says to Cyrus His anointed,
>
> whose right hand I have grasped to subdue nations before him, to disarm kings,
>
> to open the doors before him, so that the gates will not be shut:
>
> 'I will go before you and level the mountains;
>
> I will break down the gates of bronze and cut through the bars of iron.
>
> I will give you the treasures of darkness and the riches hidden in secret places,

so that you may know that I am the LORD, the God of Israel, who calls you by name.

For the sake of Jacob, My servant, and Israel, My chosen one, I call you by name;

I have given you a title of honor, though you have not known Me.

I am the LORD, and there is no other; there is no god but Me.

I will equip you for battle, though you have not known Me,

so that all may know, from where the sun rises to where it sets,

that there is none but Me; I am the LORD, and there is no other.'"

(Nevi'im, Isaiah 45)

Once Cyrus II gained dominance over both Persia and Media, what were his next empire-building moves? The Medes had vassal governments under their control, which became part of the Persian Empire. These included Bactria (modern-day Tajikistan and Uzbekistan), Parthia (northeastern Iran), and the nomadic Saka, who roamed the Eurasian Steppe and China's Xinjiang region. Cyrus assigned satraps (governors) to rule these provinces; some were the governors already in place, while others were Cyrus's relatives.

King Croesus of Lydia in western Asia Minor tried to take advantage of the power shift by attempting to conquer Asia Minor's former Median territory. Cyrus counterattacked in a drawn-out, indecisive battle in Cappadocia. Croesus withdrew for the winter but planned to renew the war in the spring with new allies. He didn't expect Cyrus to lead his forces in a lightning strike through Lydia. Cyrus reached the capital of Sardis before Croesus had any inkling he was coming.

Croesus mustered 420,000 men and met Cyrus's forces of 196,000 Medes and Persians. Cyrus ingeniously put his three hundred camels in front; the Lydian horses had not seen or smelled camels and charged off in a panic. After a cataclysmic loss, Croesus fled inside the city, but Cyrus had six siege towers! Sardis fell in two weeks, making Lydia part of the Persian Empire. Cyrus ordered Croesus to be burned to death, but he had a change of heart and ordered the flames to be extinguished. Croesus became an advisor.

This Attica pottery depicts Croesus' execution, from which he was rescued!
https://commons.wikimedia.org/wiki/File:Kroisos_stake_Louvre_G197.jpg

Once Lydia was conquered, the Greek colony of Ionia on the Aegean coast lay wide open to Cyrus. In 547 BCE, Cyrus's powerful empire embarked on the beginnings of its clash with Greece's far-flung city-states. The shattering collapse of the Ionian League's twelve Greek city-states sent shockwaves through the Greek world. As with other lands conquered by Cyrus, the Ionians paid tribute and supplied men for the Achaemenid army but maintained some local autonomy for the next three centuries.

From 547 to 539 BCE, Cyrus campaigned against the Sogdian nomads, who roamed the lands north of Bactria, where modern-day

Uzbekistan, Tajikistan, Kazakhstan, and Kyrgyzstan meet. Once Sogdiana was conquered, it remained under Persian control until around 400 BCE. It paid a tribute of semi-precious stones, namely lapis lazuli and carnelian. Meanwhile, Cyrus's general Harpagus conquered the rest of Asia Minor, taking Lycia and Cilicia on the Mediterranean coast.

The ancient Phoenicians, whose territory stretched down the Mediterranean coast from Syria through Lebanon to Galilee, pragmatically surrendered to the Persians. Other than paying an annual tribute of 350 talents, their kings remained in power. Their maritime technology and ships proved to be an asset to the Achaemenids in the Greco-Persian Wars. The Persians annexed Elam, which had been weakened by the Assyrians and Medes, around 542 BCE.

Cyrus now turned his focus to the great Neo-Babylonian Empire, which controlled Mesopotamia, Arabia, and the Levant. In 539 BCE, his army forded the Tigris in autumn when the river was at its lowest ebb. They crossed at Opis at the northern end of the Median Wall, which had been built by Nebuchadnezzar II to keep the Medes out. The Babylonians met the Medes and Persians at the riverbank, and the ensuing battle was a brutal loss for the Babylonians.

Cyrus's troops then marched into Babylon with hardly any resistance. The army carefully protected the temples and sacred sites of the holy city, ensuring that rituals continued as usual. By taking Babylon, Cyrus was taking all of Mesopotamia, which was mainly under Babylonian control. He proclaimed himself "King of Babylon, King of Sumer and Akkad, King of the four corners of the world."

The Jewish historian Josephus wrote in the *Antiquities of the Jews* that the exiled Jews in Babylon, from at least two population-relocation programs, showed Isaiah's prophecy to Cyrus. This motivated him to allow the Jews to return to Israel and rebuild their temple.

"In the first year of King Cyrus, he issued a decree concerning the house of God in Jerusalem:

'Let the house be rebuilt as a place for offering sacrifices, and let its foundations be firmly laid. It is to be sixty cubits high and sixty cubits wide, with three layers of cut stones and one of timbers. The costs are to be paid from the royal treasury.

Furthermore, the gold and silver articles of the house of God, which Nebuchadnezzar took from the temple in Jerusalem and carried to Babylon, must also be returned to the temple in Jerusalem and deposited in the house of God.'"

(Ketuvim, Ezra 6:3-5)

Once Cyrus had control of Mesopotamia, he quickly took possession of Israel, Syria, and northern Arabia. Cyrus died at the age of seventy. He was killed in a battle against Queen Tomyris of the Massagetae, a people of the lower Eurasian Steppe. When he died in 530 BCE, his mighty Achaemenid Empire stretched from the Indus River to Asia Minor. Cyrus won the admiration of the people he conquered by respecting their religions and customs, permitting broad autonomy, and governing for his subjects' profit and advantage. He established a successful centralized administrative model through satraps (governors) of the provinces.

When Cyrus's son Cambyses ascended the throne, he set out to achieve one of his father's unfulfilled goals: conquering Egypt. In 525 BCE, he besieged the Egyptian capital of Memphis in the Nile Delta, achieving victory in ten days. He next conquered the Cyrenaica region of Libya. While consolidating Persia's new African territories, an attempted coup in Persia demanded his attention. As

Cambyses hurried home, one of his injuries became gangrenous. He died of sepsis in 522 BCE.

Cambyses was childless, so his younger brother should have succeeded him; however, he died mysteriously just before or after Cambyses's death; he was likely murdered. Rising from obscurity, Darius I (also known as Darius the Great) usurped the throne. Darius was supposedly a descendant of Achaemenes from a different line than Cyrus. He stabilized the empire, built infrastructure, and conquered northwestern India, expanding the empire to its greatest size.

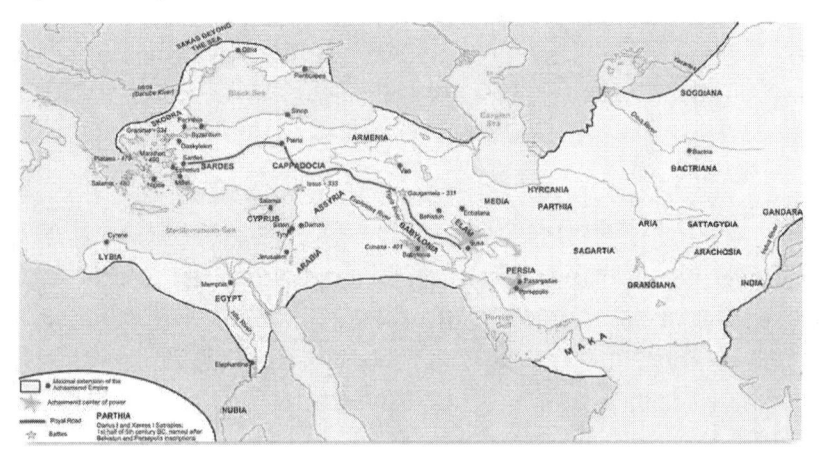

The Achaemenid Empire reached its most extensive size under Darius I.
Credit: Fabienkhan, CC BY-SA 2.5 <https://creativecommons.org/licenses/by-sa/2.5>, via Wikimedia Commons
https://commons.wikimedia.org/wiki/File:Map_achaemenid_empire_en.png

In 499 BCE, Ionia allied with the Greek city-states of Athens and Eretria, sacking and burning Sardis in a rebellion against the Persians. King Darius's troops massacred most of the Greek forces outside of Ephesus, and the Ionian insurrection imploded. But Darius seethed with rage against Greece's Eretria and Athens for intruding in his empire's affairs, and he vowed revenge. In 492 BCE, he invaded Thrace and Macedonia, adding them to the Persian Empire, then set sail for Greece. But a brutal storm obliterated most of his ships, forcing him to limp home to Persia.

While rebuilding his fleet, Darius sent his delegates to all the Greek city-states, demanding they submit to the Achaemenid Empire. All the city-states capitulated, except Sparta and Athens. Infuriated, Darius sailed across the Aegean in 490 BCE. He flattened Eritrea, then landed in Marathon, twenty-five miles from Athens. The Athenians marched across the Attica Peninsula to meet Darius in Marathon, knowing its mountainous, swampy terrain would render Darius's cavalry useless, as they would be unable to easily maneuver. Sinking in the quagmire and unnerved by the Greek hoplite battle formation, the Persians panicked and fled, losing 6,400 soldiers to the Greek's 203 casualties.

Darius's son, Xerxes I, vowed to avenge his father's humiliating loss to Athens. While preparing for his campaign, his Phoenician engineers accomplished an astonishing feat. They built a one-mile bridge over the Hellespont (the Dardanelles Strait), which allowed Xerxes's massive army to march overland to Greece. The engineers constructed a two-span bridge over the 180-foot-deep waterway by lashing 674 ships together, then building a wooden-plank bridge over the ships' decks.

Xerxes's bridge over the Dardanelles spanned one mile over stormy, churning water.
https://commons.wikimedia.org/wiki/File:Construction_of_Xerxes_Bridge_of_boats_by_Phoenician_sailors.jpg

But then a fierce storm hit, breaking the bridge into pieces. Xerxes was furious; he ordered the engineers to be decapitated, then punished the recalcitrant waterway itself, branding it with red-hot irons and beating it with three hundred lashes! The Phoenicians reassembled the bridge, and the enormous army crossed over to Europe, heading toward Greece. Meanwhile, a Persian fleet of 1,200 ships sailed across the Aegean.

No Greek city-states offered opposition until Xerxes came to the Thermopylae Pass, where seven thousand men from Sparta, Thespiae, and Thebes blocked the narrow fifty-foot-wide mountain pass guarding southern Greece. The Greek coalition held off the large Persian army for two days, fighting to the last man. After getting through the pass, Xerxes swiftly gained control of mainland Greece but received the troubling news that two savage storms had sunk two-thirds of his fleet.

Meanwhile, the Athenians abandoned their city, fleeing to the island of Salamis, where they joined up with the Greek fleet that had withdrawn to the island. Xerxes commanded what was left of his fleet, four hundred ships, to sail to Salamis. Queen Artemisia of Halicarnassus, one of Xerxes's naval commanders, warned him against fighting in the straits. Xerxes was confident that his ships would win the day and ignored her concerns.

Xerxes didn't know that three hundred Greek ships were hiding out of sight behind an island. Once his fleet entered the strait, the Greek ships surrounded him. Singing a triumphant hymn to Apollo, they crushed the Persian ships with their battering rams. Corpses and the remains of wrecked ships floated in the water as the Greeks plowed into one Persian vessel after another. The Salamis victory was a watershed moment. The Persians had been the aggressors up to this point, and now they switched to the defensive.

With winter approaching and trouble stirring back home, a demoralized Xerxes returned to Persia, never to return to Greece.

He hurried back to crush a revolt in Babylon. Several years later, Xerxes was dead, assassinated by his bodyguard commander in 465 BCE. His son Artaxerxes made no more attempts to expand Persia's hegemony over Greece. His cupbearer Nehemiah and the Jewish priest Ezra both recorded Artaxerxes's generous and kind demeanor toward his subjects. Artaxerxes consolidated and organized the massive Persian Empire throughout his long reign.

What was the significance of Persia's monumental rise in the ancient world? The Achaemenid Empire's surging ascent under Cyrus's rule profoundly impacted world history. Iran's literature, philosophy, and religions played a commanding role in global affairs for the next thousand years. The Achaemenid Empire and the two Persian dynasties that followed revered Cyrus as their father and a role model in leadership.

This brilliant founder of a soaring empire deeply impressed the Greeks. Xenophon praised Cyrus's keen administrative abilities and heroism in war. After reading Xenophon's *Cyropaedia* as a child, Alexander the Great was entranced by Cyrus and Persia. Even though Alexander conquered Persia, he set himself up as the next Cyrus, wearing Persian clothing, adopting Persian customs, and setting up his center of operations in Persia. He never returned home to Macedonia.

The Achaemenid Empire greatly impacted the cultural identity and heritage of the Middle East, Asia, and Europe. At its zenith, the empire reigned over an unprecedented 44 percent of the global population, influencing future empires' structure and development. The genius administrative model of the Achaemenid Empire served as a prototype for the Greek and Roman empires.

Chapter 14 – Everyday Life in Persia

Everyday life in the Persian Empire depended on where one lived; after all, it spanned three continents and encompassed hundreds of civilizations and languages. Even the ethnic Persians practiced different customs depending on their ancestral background and assimilation with neighboring cultures. This chapter will look at empire-wide factors and others indigenous to Persia on a journey of life in the Persian Empire.

Cyrus the Great had not just one but four capitals serving as administrative centers of his massive empire. Cyrus built Pasargadae, located ninety kilometers (fifty-six miles) northeast of modern-day Shiraz, Iran. The other capital cities were Babylon, Susa (the ancient Elamite capital), and Ecbatana in western Iran. He likely moved from city to city depending on the seasons and which regions demanded his attention. The Tanakh mentions his successors living in Susa.

How did life change for people in the countries conquered by Persia? When the Persians conquered a region, the Persian king or his general might stay long enough to organize a local government and assign leaders; after that, he would generally leave the day-today administration to the satraps (governors). The people living in a newly conquered region would not experience much change in their daily lives, and they continued in their religious practices and customs.

The main change was their governments now had to pay tribute (a sort of tax) to Persia. Tribute could be in the form of money or in goods that were a specialty of the area: gemstones, metal, cloth, leather, or any number of items. Unlike the Assyrian Empire, which bled the provinces dry, the Persians' tribute system was sustainable, or at least it was until the Greco-Persian Wars drained the treasury.

This gold daric coin represented the universal currency Darius I instituted.

Credit: Classical Numismatic Group, Inc. http://www.cngcoins.com CC BY-SA 2.5 https://creativecommons.org/licenses/by-sa/2.5 via Wikimedia Commons; https://commons.wikimedia.org/wiki/File:Daric_coin_of_the_Achaemenid_Empire_(Darius_I _to_Xerxes_II).jpg

Darius the Great initiated a coordinated tax system based on each province's economy, assets, and productivity. Wealthy Babylon paid the highest tribute. It had to provide enough food to feed the army for four months and pay one thousand silver talents. India paid its tribute in gold. Egypt's vast farms in the Nile River Delta provided 120,000 measures of grain for the empire (and later served as Athens's and Rome's granaries). Egypt also paid 700 silver talents. If a conquered region proved too ungovernable, the population could be enslaved. The Persian Empire registered and charged a sales tax on the slave markets. Other tariffs on trade provided valuable income for the empire.

Life in the Persian Empire sometimes meant heavy taxes, especially after the disastrous Greco-Persian Wars decimated the Persian fleet multiple times. The military campaign also required mammoth resources and food for its large army. The territories around the empire would occasionally attempt to overthrow their Persian overlords, especially toward the end of the Achaemenid Empire when taxes were higher and the kings less benevolent. Revolts happened with increasing frequency, making the empire vulnerable to Alexander the Great's invasion.

The Persians' centralized government permitted regional autonomy by entrusting the day-to-day government of satrapies (provinces) to governors called satraps. The satraps were not necessarily Persian; they could be chosen from the local leaders. For instance, the Jewish Daniel had served as an advisor to the Babylonian kings. When Babylon fell, the Persians appointed 120 satraps to rule throughout the kingdom. Three administrators who were accountable to the king oversaw these satraps, and Daniel was one of the three (Ketuvim, Daniel 6).

Within a satrapy (province or region), the satrap (governor) was the administrator. Under him, a military general recruited, trained, and organized a local army, and a state secretary maintained records. The general and secretary reported to both the satrap and central government. Each satrap had a measure of independence; however, royal inspectors would travel around the empire as the king's eyes and ears to learn of local situations. The main concern was ensuring the satrap's loyalty to the central government and tax compliance.

With an empire stretching across three continents and holding almost half the world's population, transportation and communication were crucial for keeping the central government abreast of what was happening around the empire. Darius I (Darius the Great) linked the satrapies with a 1,553-mile (2,500-kilometer) highway with roadside inns for merchant caravans and other travelers. It also had relay stations for the Persian postal service. The switch from clay tablets to parchment scrolls made for a much lighter load for the Persian postmen.

By changing out horses and riders, a message could travel the 1,553 miles of highway in just seven days! Chiseled in gray granite over the doors of today's Eighth Avenue New York City Post Office is Herodotus's praise of the Persian postal service: "Neither snow, nor rain, nor heat, nor gloom of night stays these courageous couriers from the swift completion of their appointed rounds."

The 5th-century BCE "Immortal" warriors wore distinctive uniforms.
Credit: Pergamon Museum, CC BY 2.0 https://creativecommons.org/licenses/by/2.0 via Wikimedia Commons;
https://commons.wikimedia.org/wiki/File:Persian_warriors_from_Berlin_Museum.jpg

Cyrus realized his vast empire needed a professional army to maintain order over internal power struggles, protect the people from external threats, and conquer new lands. His powerful full-time land army of over 100,000 men was the first to wear standard uniforms of bright colors. He recruited men to serve in his military as he conquered new lands. Various regions produced an array of exceptional soldiers with specialized military skills, such as archers, swordsmen, cavalrymen, camel-riders, elephant mahouts, and javelin throwers.

The empire had an elite military unit. Striking fear into their opponents, the elite Immortals were a specially-trained band of exactly ten thousand heavy infantrymen. A trained replacement would immediately step in if a soldier were sick, seriously wounded, or killed in battle. Under their tunics, the Immortals wore scale armor—small plates or scales (of metal, leather, or horn) sewn to leather or cloth shirts (and sometimes pants) in overlapping rows. They carried wicker shields and wielded daggers, swords, and short spears. They strapped a quiver of arrows on their back and carried a bow hooked over their shoulder.

The *sparabara* warriors were Persians trained in war from childhood. These men usually fought during the military season instead of in the year-round standing army. When not fighting, they were herdsmen and farmers. They wore quilted linen armor and carried two-meter-long spears and wicker shields. The shields effectively fended off arrows but were no match for the Greek hoplites' eighteen-foot sarissas (5.5-meter pikes). However, the *sparabara* effectively fought non-Greek forces.

The Persian military was renowned for its astonishing archers. The Elamites, Medes, Persians, and Scythians were skilled in the deadly three-bladed, socketed, copper alloy arrowheads. Their invincible charioteers, lethal cavalry, camels, and war elephants terrified their opponents. And let's not forget the incredible Phoenician maritime engineers. Xerxes's boat bridge across the Dardanelles Strait wasn't a one-off; Darius had built a similar bridge across the Bosporus.

The Persians were accustomed to fighting on land, but as their empire stretched into Europe and Africa, they realized they needed a navy. Darius the Great recruited seasoned sea warriors from Sidon and other Phoenician cities, as well as Egypt and Greece. The Phoenicians were master shipbuilders and skilled in naval war maneuvers. They built forty-meter-long ships that could carry three hundred troops. The Persians also used smaller ships to patrol large rivers like the Indus, Nile, and Tigris. The vessels had miniature siege engines to launch missiles at their opponents.

Did Xerxes really have a million men in his army when he invaded Greece? Various Greek sources, including Herodotus and Simonides the poet, reported one to three million, including the navy and non-combatants like drivers and cooks. Was this possible? Let's remember that the Achaemenid Empire held 49.4 million of about 112.4 million people globally. With such a vast population, one million military men is a possibility. But the logistics of feeding and moving that many men from Asia to Europe are almost inconceivable. They did say it took a week to cross the boat bridge over the Dardanelles.

By 400 BCE, Persians began using yakhchāls to cool food and ice.
Credit: Pastaitaken, CC BY-SA 3.0 https://creativecommons.org/licenses/by-sa/3.0, via Wikimedia Commons;
https://commons.wikimedia.org/wiki/File:Yakhchal_of_Yazd_province.jpg

An essential part of daily life is eating and drinking, and the Persians reveled in both. They built underground chambers insulated with mud and bricks to keep their food cool in the hot desert climate. Their diet was similar to the Mesopotamian civilizations; they ate mutton, fish, yogurt, bread, and a vast array of fruits and vegetables. But the Persians insisted on desserts! They scoffed at the Greeks for not eating sweets at the end of the meal, saying they were leaving the table hungry.

The Persian court was infamous for its absurdly lavish lifestyle. King Darius III traveled with an entourage of three hundred cooks and seventy wine-filterers. Birthdays were occasions for elaborate feasts. The Persians were fond of their wine and scandalized the Greeks by drinking it full strength (the Greeks watered theirs down). Herodotus wrote about Persian rulers:

> "If a crucial decision is to be made, they discuss the question when they are drunk, and the following day, the master of the house where the discussion was held submits their decision for reconsideration when they are sober. It is adopted if they still approve it; if not, it is abandoned. Conversely, any decision they make when sober is reconsidered afterward when they are drunk."

What was the Persian social structure like? They followed a hierarchal system, with the king and his extensive royal family at the top, priests and magi next, then the satraps and other nobles, military commanders and the Immortals, merchants, artisans and craftspeople, peasants, and enslaved people. The color of clothing labeled some social classes. For instance, warriors wore red, priests wore white, and shepherds wore blue. The magi were a priestly caste in Persia and Babylon, known as astrologers, seers, and exceptional scholars.

The Persians honored those of higher status by bowing to them. They didn't just bow their heads or go down on one knee; they went flat on their faces before the king and other superiors and would kiss the earth or their superior's sandals. When Alexander the Great conquered Persia, he had a bout of megalomania and began demanding his Greek military officers and others to prostrate themselves before him. The Greeks were used to democracy and thought Alexander was deranged.

Women's status in the Persian Empire seemed higher than in the Assyrian and Babylonian cultures. They were active in public life, worked alongside men for the same wages, and occasionally held supervisory positions. Some queens were even warriors. One example was Queen Artemisia of Halicarnassus, which was a Greek colony in present-day Turkey that had come under Persian rule. Herodotus, who was also from Halicarnassus, noted the respect that the Persian king Xerxes had for her advice when she commanded five ships in Xerxes's fleet against Greece. Xerxes praised her for excelling over the other naval officers.

The Persians were notable for their tolerance of minorities. Cyrus the Great proclaimed the lack of prejudice for all ethnicities, religions, and languages throughout the empire on the clay Cyrus Cylinder. The Achaemenid Empire's ethnic and religious minorities continued practicing their faiths and cultures without interference. Cyrus even helped fund the Jews' return to Jerusalem from the Babylonian exile to rebuild their temple.

What did Persians wear? The men were vain about their appearance. They wore kohl eyeliner, used hot irons to curl their hair and beards, and anointed their hair and skin with scented oils. Cyrus's Jewish administrator Daniel mentioned going on a three-week religious fast, which included not anointing himself with oil.

While most men in Mesopotamia and nearby civilizations wore knee-length or ankle-length tunics, the Persian men started wearing pants and leggings, especially in the military, where tunics could be restricting. A typical male outfit might have included a tall cylindrical cap, close-fitting trousers and jacket, a long-sleeved coat, and leather shoes or boots tied with laces. Other men's headgear included a turban or a long scarf draped around the head.

Persian men wore a variety of headgear, clothing, and shoes.
https://commons.wikimedia.org/wiki/File:Ancient_Times,_Persian._-_007_-_Costumes_of_All_Nations_(1882).JPG

Women wore ankle-length tunics or pleated dresses. They wore a single braid and something like today's chador: a large scarf covering the head and neck but leaving their face uncovered. Cotton was cultivated in Mesopotamia during this era, and Persians liked to dye their material in bright colors and wear luxurious scarves, multiple layers, and eye-catching earrings and pendants. Silk from China was a prized trade item and a favorite fabric of the nobility.

What languages did the Persians speak? Up through Darius the Great's reign, Elamite, with an Old Persian language influence, was the spoken and written language for the chancellery and the empire's administration. Elam was located in western Iran on the Persian Gulf and had previously dominated Iran and northern Mesopotamia. Carved inscriptions on monuments and seals were usually trilingual, containing the Old Persian, Elamite, and Akkadian languages. Akkadian was the commonly spoken language in Persia. Persian cuneiform developed under Darius the Great, mixing alphabetic, logogram, and syllabic symbols. Aramaic continued as the lingua franca (common language) for reading and writing in Mesopotamia and the Levant.

When considering the religious beliefs of Persia, we cannot forget how the Persians valued the virtue of truth. Regardless of which gods they worshiped, integrity and honesty shone through as the epitome of a righteous individual. Herodotus recorded that Persian boys concentrated on learning three things: horse-riding, archery, and speaking the truth. He said the Persians believed the biggest disgrace was lying. Next in line was being in debt, which caused problems on many fronts, but the biggest issue was that a debtor tended to lie. The Achaemenid Persians considered lying a cardinal sin, sometimes even punishable by death. This concept predated the Persians, as Hammurabi's code included the death penalty for false witnesses and false accusers.

In the Achaemenid period, Zoroastrianism spread to southwestern Iran, influencing the Persian leadership and becoming a defining cultural element. Along with the ancient Vedic deities from the east, Zoroastrianism encompassed the concepts and gods of the ancient Iranian pantheon; they became minor deities or something like angels. This syncretism helped spur the broad acceptance of Zoroastrianism throughout Iran, allowing it to gain the patronage of Persian kings.

The Achaemenid-era relief pictures the struggle between good (the king) and evil (the lion-griffin creature), representing Zoroastrian dualism.

Credit: Bernard Gagnon, CC BY-SA 4.0 https://creativecommons.org/licenses/by-sa/4.0 via Wikimedia Commons; https://commons.wikimedia.org/wiki/File:Zoroastrian_Fire_Temple,_Yazd_03.jpg

Beginning with Darius the Great, perhaps earlier, the imperial patronage of Zoroastrianism made it effectively the state religion throughout the empire. However, the Persian kings continued to exercise the broad tolerance of all faiths, something that Cyrus the Great had initiated. For instance, Cyrus directed Persia's treasurer, Mithredath, to count out all the articles Nebuchadnezzar had looted from the Jewish temple and placed in Marduk's Babylonian temple. Cyrus returned these to Sheshbazzar, Prince of Judah.

Even though Darius the Great was Zoroastrian, he intervened on behalf of the Jews who came into conflict with the Babylonians and other people. The Assyrians had relocated them to Israel over a hundred years earlier. The issue was rebuilding Jerusalem's temple, which had begun in Cyrus's reign, but the local non-Jewish leadership in Israel stopped the construction. Darius ordered the cost of rebuilding the Jewish temple to be paid for from the royal treasury of the provinces west of the Euphrates. He also mandated sacrificial animals and food for the priests so they could offer sacrifices and pray for Darius and his family.

In the later Achaemenid Empire, Zoroastrian worship became much less monotheistic. Berossus, a Chaldean priest of Marduk and a historian, wrote that Artaxerxes II Mnemon, who reigned from 405 to 358 BCE, began making cult statues of the Zoroastrian lesser deities. This was the first time that idols appeared in Persian temples. Both Herodotus and Berossus reported that the Persians had not previously prayed to images of the gods.

A trilingual inscription in Susa preserved Artaxerxes's prayers to Ahura Mazda, Anahita, and Mithra. He elevated the worship of Anahita, goddess of water, fertility, wisdom, and healing, by erecting temples and images of her in Babylon, Ecbatana, and Susa. The Persian Sasanian dynasty repaired and decorated these temples five hundred years later.

The daily lives of ancient Persians in the Achaemenid Empire included a rich and diverse culture that respected all religions and where multiple ethnicities lived together and learned from each other. Speaking the truth was a highly valued virtue; the Greeks and others outside the empire admired the Persians' honesty. Persian culture enriched the lives of people around the realm and beyond.

Chapter 15 – Persian Art, Architecture, and Technology

Ancient Persia produced a rich heritage of art, architecture, and technological innovations that has captured the imagination and encouraged new techniques for thousands of years. Its intricate and enchanting architecture, ceramics, painting, metalworking, and sculptures graced palaces, temples, and even ordinary homes. By exploring Persian inventions, we get an insight into their way of life.

Before the nomadic Persians arrived on the Iranian Plateau, other civilizations lived there that had a rich and distinctive culture, which helped shape Persian art and architecture. Influences of the older cultures of Elam and Susiana and the neighboring civilizations of Sumer, Babylon, Assyria, and Akkad all blended into a novel milieu of creative beauty. Herodotus commented, "The Persians adopt more foreign customs than anyone else."

The Persians had a true knack for embracing and assimilating other cultures and concepts and then putting their stamp on them by improving and taking them to a higher level. When Cyrus the Great established the Achaemenid Empire, he appreciated the ancient cultures of his own land and those he conquered. He encouraged innovations in art, architecture, and technology, developing a brilliant and distinctive Persian style in the process.

This reproduction of the ornate pillars and roof of Persepolis's Apadana is an example of elaborate Persian architecture.

https://commons.wikimedia.org/wiki/File:Persepolis_Reconstruction_Apadana_Toit_Chipiez.JPEG

Before the Medes and Persians arrived in the Iranian Plateau, nomadic people had put down roots, establishing Susa in the lower Zagros Mountains. And before they came, the Elamites were already there, east of Sumer and down along the Persian Gulf. The people of Susa and Elam interacted with each other and with the Sumerians and the Zagros Mountain tribes. Eventually, the mountain tribes and the plateau tribes united to form a sophisticated urban state.

Eventually, King Eannatum (circa 2500-2400 BCE) and other Sumerian kings established hegemony over Elam, influencing Elamite art, such as statuettes of human worshipers representing communal devotion. Akkadian and Sumerian cylinder seals shaped Elamite depictions of gods and humans, which were motifs the Persians would later adopt and develop. The Persian Empire's artists drew on these past artistic elements and refined them.

Sargon of Akkad conquered today's Iran in the late 3rd millennium and implemented further advances in syncretizing art and architectural motifs. Persian architecture was an eclectic blending of multiple cultures that had a distinctive Persian identity. The Akkadian influence was dramatically displayed in Chogha Zanbil: a massive complex built during the reign of Elamite King Untash-Napirisha, circa 1340 BCE. Its brick ziggurat with a temple on top is relatively well preserved over three thousand years later.

A stunning example of Achaemenid architecture and art is the Persepolis ruins near the southern Zagros Mountains, which date back to 515 BCE. Cyrus the Great selected the remote location for the Persian ceremonial capital or religious center and thoughtfully developed its stately design. But Darius the Great began the construction of Persepolis's terraces and palaces, and his son Xerxes completed most of Persepolis.

One of Persepolis's first structures was the Apadana: the opulent main hall of the kings, where they received tribute from the nations and bestowed gifts on their subjects. Twenty-meter-high columns supported the roof, with figures of bulls adorning the columns' capitals. Two colossal stairways rose to the hall on the north and east, decorated with reliefs depicting men in the costumes of the empire's nations. Magnificently landscaped gardens surrounded the Apadana.

Not only did Darius oversee the early construction of Persepolis, but the incredibly ambitious king also rebuilt his summer capital of Susa, following Cyrus's design of elaborate gardens and erecting a breathtaking palace complex. Both Persepolis and Susa featured animals, such as birds, bulls, and lions, at the tops of columns. They were also etched into the borders of the roofs. The slender columns drew the eye upward to the colorful and intricate designs around the ceiling, which was built with planks from the cedars of Lebanon.

This lamassu-like creature decorated the wall of Darius's palace.
https://commons.wikimedia.org/wiki/File:Sphinx_Darius_Louvre.jpg

Darius decorated his palace with enameled terracotta reliefs of lions, archers, unicorns, double bulls, palms, flowers, and bells. The reliefs' brightly colored dyes gave a lifelike quality to the images. Perhaps the most eye-catching is a relief of a creature with a man's head, a lion's body, and an eagle's wings, something like a *lamassu* or griffin.

Was the unicorn real or mythical?

Credit: Mohammad.m.nazari, CC BY-SA 4.0 https://creativecommons.org/licenses/by-sa/4.0 via Wikimedia Commons; https://commons.wikimedia.org/wiki/File:Unicorn_in_Apadana,_Shush,_Iran--2017-10.jpg

A spectacular image of a unicorn graced the wall of the Apadana in Susa. A relief set on blue-glazed tile portrayed the white, horse-like creature with a spiral horn, a tail like a lion, and wings of an eagle. Did the Persians consider the unicorn a mythical creature or a real animal? We do not have any written Persian accounts of unicorns, but Greek natural history authors believed they were real animals that lived in India. Many seals from Bronze-Age India show a single-horned animal looking more like a cow than a horse. Ctesias, a Greek physician living in Persia during the Achaemenid Empire, described unicorns as wild asses with black, red, or white coats and a horn that was a cubit and a half (twenty-eight inches).

An important example of Achaemenid art is the reliefs decorating the stairs of Persepolis's Apadana hall. On the northern panel, the king (probably Darius the Great) receives a distinguished official performing a greeting ritual of blowing a kiss. Typically, everyone was required to prostrate themselves before the king, face to the floor, and kiss his feet or kiss the ground (as in, "I worship the ground you stand on"). This official is standing and blowing a kiss to the king, indicating his high rank.

Along the other walls of the stairs, more sets of reliefs portray the people of the vast empire's regions lined up to offer tribute to the king. They can be identified by their clothing: Medes, Elamites, Armenians, Parthians, Babylonians, Lydians, Syrians, Cappadocians, Sacae, Greeks, Bactrians, Indians, and on and on. A hippopotamus is shown roaming around. He's with the Egyptians, so perhaps he was part of the tribute.

The relief's history is intriguing. At some point, the reliefs on the northern stairs with the king were removed and placed in the treasury, where they stayed until archaeologists dug them up over two thousand years later.

This section of the enormous relief from the Apadana Hall in Persepolis shows Lydians offering tribute. The official (with the knife in his belt) leads the first man by the hand, implying an amicable relationship between the king and the conquered people.

Credit: Darfash Kaviani, CC BY-SA 3.0 https://creativecommons.org/licenses/by-sa/3.0, via Wikimedia Commons; https://commons.wikimedia.org/wiki/File:Apadana_Persepolis_Iran.JPG

Perhaps the best-known art collection of the Achaemenid Empire is the Oxus treasure, a hoard of crafted gold and silver treasures found near and in the Oxus River, where it separates modern-day Tajikistan and Afghanistan. The treasure dates to the

Achaemenid period, when the region belonged to the First Persian Empire. In 1880, a Russian newspaper reported that locals had found treasure in the ruins of the ancient fort of Takht-i Kuwad and in the river itself. These priceless items had been scattered in the sand, exposed by the dry season.

The finds included exquisite bowls, coins, figurines, jewelry, jugs, and gold plaques. Scholars believe they may have once adorned a nearby temple, and the priests hid them for safekeeping during a tumultuous political period. The stunning and complex craftsmanship demonstrates tremendous metallurgy skill, especially in a miniature golden chariot and horses with riders. The fine detail required exceptional skill and reflected Egyptian influence.

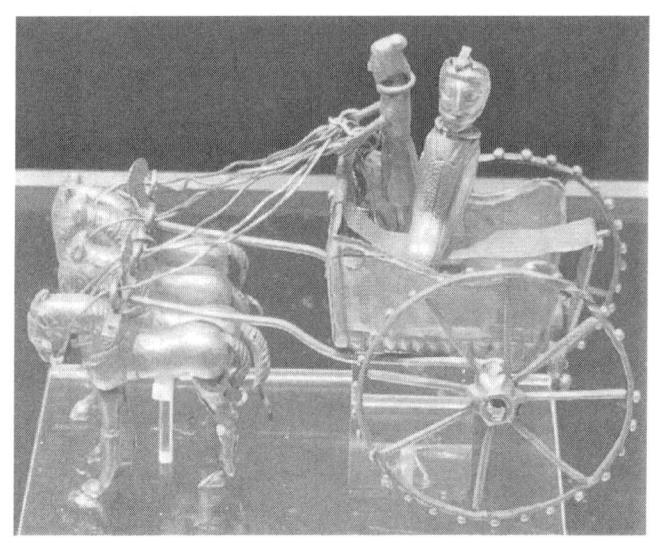

This Oxus golden chariot displays incredible craftsmanship.
Credit: BabelStone, CC BY-SA 3.0 https://creativecommons.org/licenses/by-sa/3.0 via Wikimedia Commons; https://commons.wikimedia.org/wiki/File:Oxus_chariot_model.jpg

These exquisite pieces may have been cut from sheet gold. The craftsmanship is so realistic that the chariot wheels would have freely turned when created thousands of years ago. The chariot shows signs of repair in ancient times. Four horses pull the chariot, which carries two figures: a driver and a seated passenger. Handrails are attached to the chariot's rear to assist with stepping in and out. The front of the chariot has the image of Bes, the Egyptian dwarf god.

The Oxus treasure represents what must have been an enormous production of precious-metal work in the Achaemenid period. As the Persian Empire exploded in all directions, conquering regions from India to Greece to Egypt, it swallowed up the artistic hubs of the ancient world. As the Persians assimilated creative skills and techniques from these areas, they developed a unique Persian style, such as the griffin-headed gold bracelets from Oxus pictured in the 5th-century Persepolis reliefs and which Xenophon described as gifts of honor in the Achaemenid court.

The Oxus treasure trove included multiple silver and gold figurines. Some of them probably represent worshipers rather than deities. One silver and gold figure is wearing a headdress, suggesting he is a king. A larger silver statuette shows a nude young man wearing a gold conical hat. Scholars believe this figure has Greek influences, as nude art was not typical of Persia.

Entrancing armlets, bracelets, and neck torcs are adorned with animal heads: bulls, ducks, goats, ibex, lions, sheep, and mythical creatures like griffins. The griffin-headed bracelets required complex manufacturing since several elements are soldered together. Although most are now missing, their inlays held jewels in their original state. The jewelry hints at Assyrian and Egyptian influences. Other jewelry includes signet rings and cylinder seals.

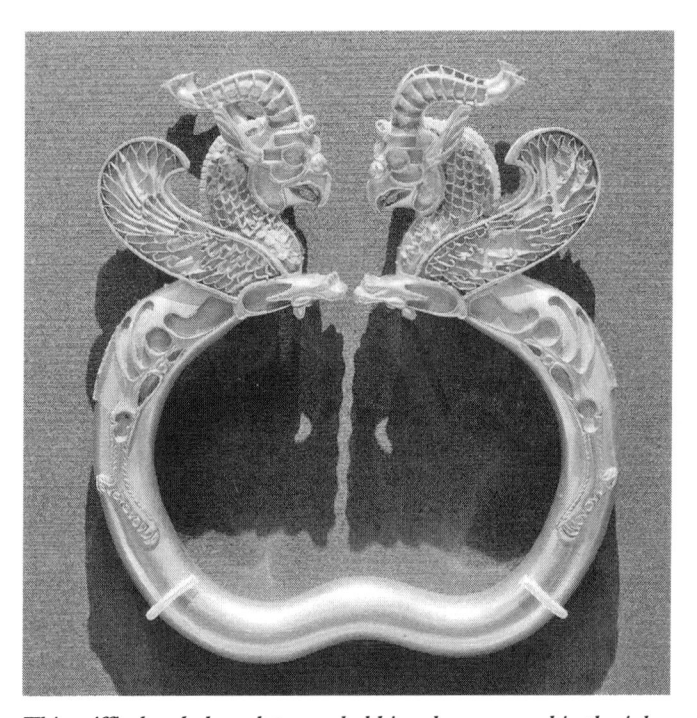

This griffin-headed armlet once held jewels or enamel in the inlay.

https://commons.wikimedia.org/wiki/File:Armlet_from_the_Oxus_Treasure_BM_1897.12-31.116.jpg

The Oxus treasure includes a lion-griffin gold plaque with an ibex's body and a leaf-shaped tail. The position of the creature suggests a Scythian influence. Two prongs at the back of the piece imply it was an ornament worn on a cap or adorning someone's hair. Like tribute vessels pictured in the Persepolis reliefs, a leaping ibex carving probably once served as a vase handle.

Before the Persians arrived in Iran, the Elamites produced eye-catching pottery: bowls, cups, and pots in striking geometric shapes or depicting ibex and other animals. They also made numerous clay figurines of beguiling animals: rabbits, cows, and dogs—many dogs. The animals may have represented people in Aesop-like fables. One almost life-sized clay cow found at the entrance to the Chogha Zanbil ziggurat, circa 1250 BCE, was dedicated to the god Inshushinak.

This realistic piebald pottery cow exemplifies Elamite art.

Credit: Fabienkhan, CC BY-SA 2.5 https://creativecommons.org/licenses/by-sa/2.5 via Wikimedia Commons; https://commons.wikimedia.org/wiki/File:Iran_bastan_19_-_pottery_cow_-_Chogha_zanbil.jpg

Pottery from the Achaemenid period includes excavated pieces dating from Darius the Great's reign (521-486 BCE). This pottery is distinctly less ornate than Elamite ceramics. It featured eggshell, white, reddish, and yellow glazes on bowls, jars, and cylindrical amphorae, reflecting central and southern Mesopotamian influences. Painted pottery was rare; the few painted ceramics featured red paint on buff-colored pottery. Some of the Achaemenid-era pottery dating to the 6th to 5th centuries BCE appeared mass-produced for everyday utilitarian use.

Metal or ceramic festoon-ware was distinctive in Persia beginning in the Achaemenid era: drinking vessels of bronze, copper, gold, or silver or pottery with an animal head. They were probably used for special occasions like ceremonial court banquets. In their nomadic days, Persians drank wine from animal horns, which evolved into ornate drinking vessels resembling a horn with an animal head. These fascinating vessels spread throughout the empire and to Greece.

This mountain-goat drinking horn from Anatolia dates to 500–400 BCE.
Credit: Dosseman, CC BY-SA 4.0 https://creativecommons.org/licenses/by-sa/4.0 *via* Wikimedia Commons; https://commons.wikimedia.org/wiki/File:Ankara_Archaeology_and_art_museum_Rhyton_Bronze_Achaemenid_Persian_500-400_BC_2019_3473.jpg

Another example of Achaemenid-era pottery is dotted Triangle Ware, which dates to the 5th and 4th centuries BCE and is found in northwestern Persia and central Anatolia. Potters produced them from local clays, and they have a well-smoothed surface. They feature vertical and horizontal bands forming panels decorated with animal, floral, or geometric motifs with ladder or chevron patterns on the vessel rims. Triangles were the dominant decoration, hence the name. They were painted bold orange, red, purple, and mahogany brown. They apparently formed table sets with bowls, jugs, and other ceramics.

Persians began working with glass starting in the Late Bronze Age. Archaeologists found glass beads in the Dinkha Tepe site in Iranian Azerbaijan. They found glass tubes from the Elamite period at Chogha Zanbil and Iron Age mosaic glass cups in northern Iran, reflecting Mesopotamian influences. Glassware from the Achaemenid period includes glass tubes holding kohl in Azerbaijan and Kurdistan.

In addition to delightful art and architecture, the Persians produced intriguing innovations in technology and other fields. Water sources are always a concern in arid and semi-arid regions. This led to the development of the qanat irrigation system, which brought water from an aquifer or well up to the surface using an underground aqueduct. This ancient qanat irrigation system permitted water transport over long distances without losing much water to evaporation in the hot, dry climate. Another advantage was its resistance to earthquakes, floods, or wartime destruction by enemies.

Unlike the Mesopotamian irrigation systems, which were fed from rivers, the qanat system used underground water. Thus, it did not depend on rainfall levels and delivered a relatively reliable flow even during times of drought. It was built with vertical shafts at intervals, similar to shaft wells, and connected to a sloping tunnel, drawing the water up from the aquafers. The qanat system turned deserts into farmland and provided a water source for the Persians' lush gardens in their cities and palaces.

The Persians invented the world's first known windmill as early as 134 BCE and perhaps even earlier. They used this used to pump water or grind grain. They used wicker paddles woven from reeds or fabric sails. They attached four to eight wicker paddles or cloth sails to a central axis in a panemone design (with a vertical rotating axis and the sails or paddles moving parallel to the wind). As the wind blew the sails, this turned the axle, which was connected to a water-transportation device or grain grinders.

Using ancient Persian technology, these towers are windcatchers in today's Yazd, Iran. An "ab anbar" (water reservoir) is in the middle.

Credit: Diego Delso, CC BY-SA 4.0 https://creativecommons.org/licenses/by-sa/4.0 via Wikimedia Commons Diego Delso, CC BY-SA 4.0 https://creativecommons.org/licenses/by-sa/4.0 via Wikimedia Commons;
https://commons.wikimedia.org/wiki/File:Edificios_en_Yazd,_Ir%C3%A1n,_2016-09-21,_DD_17.jpg

Persia had cool or cold winters (depending on the location), but the summer heat could be brutal: over 100°F (38°C) on some scorching days. This propelled the enterprising Persians to devise ways of staying cool. They developed windcatchers or wind towers, which are still used today. These provided natural ventilation and passive cooling. The windcatchers drew the cooler air down and pushed the stifling air up and out, maintaining a somewhat comfortable indoor temperature.

Egypt had established hospitals in the Old Kingdom (2613-2181 BCE), and the Babylonians had a well-developed medical system. But the Persians developed the world's first teaching hospital. Even before that happened, the Persians had a deep respect for medical science; for instance, Darius the Great restored the medical books and equipment at the Sais medical school in Egypt.

But the innovators of the Persian Sassanian Empire took the medical concepts in place and developed a teaching hospital with a library and medical school. Azadokht Shahbanu, the wife of King Shapur (r. 240-270 CE), brought Greek physicians to the royal court to establish a teaching hospital where experienced physicians could train new doctors. The Academy of Gundeshapur became the region's premier intellectual center. One of the requirements for graduation was to cure three patients. Doctors' fees were on a sliding scale depending on the patient's income.

Ancient Persians worked hard and fought hard, but they enjoyed taking time to unwind with friends and family, which is an essential part of any culture. They loved throwing banquets and birthday parties. They developed animation for amusement at these gatherings; they would have a cup painted with successive scenes around it, so it looked like the picture on the cup was moving when they turned it. One example is a ram jumping into the air to catch leaves from a tree in his mouth. The Persians also enjoyed singing to stringed instruments like the *tar*, the prototype for today's guitar.

Ancient Persia brought multiple cultures from three continents under its dominion; it was the most expansive empire at that time. Through respecting and encouraging individual cultures and blending them, the distinctive Persian culture emerged as a driving force in art, architecture, and technical innovations. Although Islamic Arabs initially suppressed Persian culture, it endured and later became a decisive influence on Islamic culture. Today, we enjoy and appreciate the vibrant Persian contributions to art, architecture, and technology as people continue to rework ancient customs and innovations with a unique Persian spin.

Chapter 16 – Persia's Great Enemy: Alexander the Great

Everything was ready! Philip II of Macedon had spent years fighting the Greeks, ending their incessant internecine conflicts and molding them into one united front, something no one thought possible. Philip was now poised to launch his stupendous Greek coalition forces against Persia. An advance force of ten thousand men was already in Asia Minor, preparing to free the Greek city-states from Persian hegemony.

Nothing could stop him now. Nothing that was except murder. While Philip was celebrating his daughter's wedding, Philip's bodyguard and former lover Pausanias suddenly pulled out his dagger and plunged it into Philip's ribs.

It was 336 BCE. Over two hundred years had passed since Cyrus formed the mighty Achaemenid Empire. The Persian Empire's control over multiple Greek city-states along Asia Minor's Ionian coast was a bone of contention for the Ionian Greeks and the mainland Greeks, who were accustomed to freely trading with their ancient relatives. The Persians impeded their seafaring trade.

The Persians had invaded Thrace, Macedonia, and Greece under Darius the Great. But Darius and his son Xerxes I were defeated multiple times by storms at sea, by the Spartans' intransigence, and by the Athenians' cunning naval strategies. When the southern Greek states stopped fighting each other and formed a united front against Xerxes's large army, they won!

The loss was catastrophic for the Achaemenid Empire. The costly Greco-Persian Wars had depleted Persia's treasury. And the Ionian-Greek city-states revolted again. When Xerxes's son Artaxerxes I ascended the throne, he initiated a new strategy. Instead of military action against Greece, he endeavored to weaken the Athens-led southern Greek coalition by funding their rival Greek city-states.

Artaxerxes's ploy worked. The Greek coalition began unraveling, and the southern Greek states started fighting each other again in the Peloponnesian Wars. While fighting Sparta, Athens sent two hundred ships to aid Egypt and Libya in a revolt against their Persian overlords. Although Athens fared well against Sparta, it received appalling news from Egypt: the Persians had crushed the Athenian fleet. Athens forgot all about Sparta and focused on Persia, strengthening its Delian League coalition.

After several years, Athens and Sparta were back at war, which didn't go well for Athens. First, a horrible plague decimated the population. Next, the city suffered devastating losses from Sparta. Then, a coup overthrew Athens's democracy. But the commander of the Athenian fleet, Alcibiades, refused to submit to the new Athenian government. Instead, in 410 BCE, he sailed the fleet to the Hellespont, engaging Sparta and Persia and winning an astounding victory in the Battle of Cyzicus.

This triumph spurred the Athenians to restore democracy and take back the Ionian Greek city-states from Persia. But the Athenian victory was short-lived. Darius II was now ruling the Persian-Achaemenid Empire, and he supported Sparta in the struggle with Athens. With Persia's support, Sparta rebuilt its fleet and ultimately crushed Athens. In 404 BCE, Athens and its allies surrendered to Sparta, handed over their naval fleets, and gave up their tributary cities.

Meanwhile, the Persian Empire enjoyed 45 years of relative stability under Artaxerxes II, who was notable for having over 300 wives and 115 sons. Artaxerxes II invested energy and funds to improve the Persian Empire's infrastructure and build temples. But he also inserted himself into Greece's affairs. Hoping to destabilize Greece, Persia subsidized Athens, Corinth, and Thebes against Sparta. Then, in 387 BCE, Artaxerxes abandoned the Athenian coalition, took back the Greek city-states in Ionia, and gave Sparta hegemony over all of Greece. Artaxerxes prevailed over Greece, but Egypt had revolted early in his reign, and his attempt to retake Egypt in 373 BCE failed.

The year before Artaxerxes III became ruler of the Persian Empire, Philip II ascended the throne of Macedonia. This was a large but obscure and weak state north of Greece; at this time, it was on the brink of obliteration by its neighbors. But Philip II was ambitious and well-schooled in military tactics after spending his teen years in Thebes. He would soon reform his army and transform Macedonia into an empire. In his first year as king, he trounced the states surrounding Macedonia, which had been threatening to annihilate Macedonia just months earlier. He then fought his way through northern, central, and southern Greece, conquering states and forming a coalition of all of Greece except Sparta. His goal was to rid Greece of its perpetual threat by swallowing up the Persian Empire.

Meanwhile, Artaxerxes III had been busy retaking Egypt, savagely squelching a revolt in Sidon, and dealing with rebellions in Asia Minor and Cyprus. He finally got the entire Persian Empire under control and enjoyed the last six years of his reign in relative peace. But Bagoas, his favorite eunuch and commander, poisoned him. Bagoas then poisoned the next king, Artaxerxes IV, and killed all of his children. Finally, a distant relative, Darius III, ascended the throne and poisoned Bagoas out of self-preservation.

And that brings us to 336 BCE. Poison had exterminated the Persian royal family, and Philip II lay bleeding out in Macedonia. While his body was still warm, Philip's military and nobles proclaimed his son, twenty-year-old Alexander, as the next king of Macedonia. Alexander had spent his childhood being tutored by Aristotle, and he had joined his father in war for several years. Although he was young, he was an astute general and well-trained in statesmanship. Alexander was ready to step into his father's shoes and continue his mission to take on the Persian Empire.

But first, he had to quell some revolts. His father Philip had the Greek city-states all lined up to invade Persia, but with his death, Athens, Thebes, Thessaly, and Thrace began backing out. Alexander marched south with three thousand men. The Thessalian army waited for him at the pass at Mount Olympus. But Alexander circumnavigated the pass by night, climbing up and over nearby Mount Ossa. When the Thessalians woke up, he was at their rear! Shaken, the Thessalians surrendered.

This 3ᵈ-century BCE statue of Alexander is signed "Menas."

https://commons.wikimedia.org/wiki/File:Alexander_The_Great_statue_-_estatua_de_Alejandro_Magno.jpg

The rest of the city-states in southern Greece quickly bowed to his leadership, apologizing for revolting. Alexander forgave them; he needed their military strength for his quest against Persia. But now, the northern states were openly revolting, so Alexander headed north, brilliantly reining them in. However, Athens and Thebes rebelled—again! Enraged, Alexander marched back south, flattened Thebes, and sold the citizens into slavery. Aghast, Athens promptly surrendered.

Alexander now had his unified Greek coalition ready to campaign against the Achaemenid superpower in what would rank among the most spectacular military expeditions in history. Alexander's audacious Asian invasion established a vast and powerful, albeit brief, empire within ten years. The Greeks called him Alexander the Great, but he was Alexander the Accursed to the Persians.

With a forty-thousand-man army, Alexander and his proficient general, Parmenion, crossed into Asia Minor in 334 BCE. As the Persian generals tracked his approach, they discussed their strategies. One Persian general, Memnon of Rhodes, was a Greek mercenary. He advised the Persians to pursue a scorched earth strategy, in which the men would withdraw to the interior and destroy the fields and fruit trees on the way. "He'll leave if he can't feed his army!"

But the Persian generals thought it cowardly to retreat, and they weren't keen on destroying their own food sources. They decided to engage Alexander in battle at the River Granicus. The Persians lined up along the shallow river's steep banks, forcing the Greeks to wade across and climb up to meet them. Alexander's formation had the Thessalian-Thracian cavalry at the left flank and his phalanx (the soldier formation carrying shields and spears) in the middle. He joined the right flank with his specialized Macedonian cavalry, elite infantry, expert archers, and Bulgarian javelin-throwers.

The Persians looked at the setting sun and assumed the Greeks would cross the river at sunrise. But Alexander surprised them, suddenly charging his forces swiftly across the river. Under a hail of Persian arrows, Alexander's cavalry plunged through the water, then raced up the steep bank. The Persians tried to push them down the bank and back into the river, but the Greeks came at them too fast.

Alexander impaled Mithridates, Darius's son-in-law. Before he could retrieve his spear, a Persian horseman struck Alexander with his scimitar, cutting his helmet in two. Alexander jerked his javelin out of Mithridates, swung around, and plunged it into his attacker. At that moment, another Persian on horseback had his sword poised to stab Alexander in the back. But Alexander's good friend, Cleitus the Black, sliced off the Persian's arm.

Finally, the infantry waded through the river and formed a wall of formidable eighteen-foot sarissas (long pikes). The Persians had never been met by spears three times as long as they were! Panicked, they whirled around in full retreat. Alexander's first battle of the great war was a sensational victory, and Asia Minor's Greek states were now emancipated from Persia. When Alexander marched toward Lydia's capital city of Sardis, its satrap immediately surrendered.

Alexander knew he needed to shut down the Persian navy so they couldn't transport food, supplies, and men or attack his navy. Instead of attacking their ships by sea, he stormed Miletus and Halicarnassus, two important naval bases, rendering Persia's navy impotent.

Alexander then marched to Lycia and Phrygia. Gordium, Phrygia's capital, had the Gordian Knot. An oracle said that the man who untied it would be Asia's ruler. Alexander took one look at the tangle, drew his sword, and hacked it in two. He had undone the knot: Asia was his! This is, of course, a legend, so it might not have actually occurred, but it is an interesting story nonetheless.

Meanwhile, King Darius mustered a massive army and approached Alexander near Cilicia, spreading his men across the coastal plain and trapping Alexander's men against the Nur Mountains. Unperturbed, Alexander swiftly ordered his men into formation, using the same lineup at Granicus. General Parmenion was on the left with the Greek allies, the indomitable Macedonian phalanx was in the middle, and Alexander and his elite cavalry and infantry were at the right end.

The two armies lined up facing each other on opposite banks of the Pinarus River. Suddenly, Alexander charged at full speed. His horses galloped through the water, but the foot soldiers' armor and long spears slowed their crossing in the swift river. Alexander charged straight into the Persian foot soldiers with his cavalry, creating pandemonium, while the Macedonian infantry waded the river and regrouped into position.

Darius III from a Pompeii mosaic that probably copied a 3rd-century BCE painting.
Credit: Carole Raddato from Frankfurt, Germany, CC BY-SA 2.0
https://creativecommons.org/licenses/by-sa/2.0 *via* Wikimedia Commons;
https://commons.wikimedia.org/wiki/File:Darius_III_mosaic.jpg

King Darius intently scanned the battle and paled as he watched Alexander. Despite his thigh running with blood from a stab wound, Alexander heedlessly and relentlessly charged, cutting down anyone in his way. "He's insane!" Darius likely said, trembling as he watched Alexander approach.

Suddenly, the Persian king swung his chariot around and charged off the battlefield, leaving his men to fend for themselves.

Word swiftly shot through the Persian ranks that Darius had abandoned the field. They looked at each other, then at the Macedonians' bristling sarissas. Why should they be impaled by eighteen-foot pikes? They swirled around and ran! Alexander's victory at the Battle of Issus was swift and sensational. Darius didn't just leave his army behind. His mother, wife, and two daughters were at the Persian camp. Alexander took the queen-mother, the queen, and the princesses as hostages but gave them profound respect and care. He later married Princess Stateira.

One by one, the Phoenician cities on the Mediterranean coast surrendered to Alexander, further breaking Persia's Mediterranean naval power. Only the ancient city of Tyre on an island off Lebanon's shores, the fierce ruler of the sea for two thousand years, refused to concede. Alexander's engineers built a causeway to the island, and he rolled his siege engines across as the Phoenicians attacked with their fire ships. After seven months of horrendous battle, Tyre fell. At this point, King Darius sent Alexander a letter offering his friendship, his daughter in marriage, a hefty ransom to return his family, and all the territory west of the Halys River in Turkey (where the Greek colonies of Asia Minor lay). Alexander refused.

Passing out of Phoenicia on their way to Egypt, the Macedonian army approached the seemingly invincible Gaza. Alexander's engineers shook their heads. The city stood on a high hill; the siege engines couldn't reach the walls. But Alexander insisted there was a way to take the city. Finally, the engineers devised a plan of building hills alongside Gaza's hill, bringing their missile launchers high enough. While constructing the hills, an arrow shot from Gaza. It penetrated Alexander's shield, impaling his shoulder. In the end, though, Gaza fell.

The Egyptians welcomed Alexander as their deliverer from Persian rule, against which they had been revolting for decades. Their satrap handed him the keys to the treasury, and the Memphis priest crowned him as their new pharaoh. At the mouth of the Nile, Alexander founded Alexandria, a city that would soon become a brilliant Hellenistic center. Alexander visited the Oracle of Amun-Ra, who pronounced Alexander as the son of Amun, the Egyptians' chief god. Hearing this, Alexander seemed to really believe he was divine, and he expected everyone to acknowledge his celestial standing.

King Darius wrote Alexander again, thanking him for kindly caring for his mother and offering him all the territory west of the Euphrates (essentially half the empire), co-rulership, his daughter's hand in marriage, and thirty thousand talents in silver. Alexander roared in laughter. Darius's two daughters were his captives, and he wasn't settling for just half of the empire; he wanted it all! Alexander messaged Darius that Asia could only have one king. He should surrender now or prepare to fight to see who the one king would be.

Alexander fighting Darius in the Battle of Issus in a mosaic from Pompeii.

https://commons.wikimedia.org/wiki/File:Alexander_and_Bucephalus_-_Battle_of_Issus_mosaic_-_Museo_Archeologico_Nazionale_-_Naples_BW.jpg

Darius marched out to meet Alexander at Gaugamela in northern Mesopotamia with almost twice as many men, war elephants, and chariots; the Greeks were unaccustomed to fighting elephants and men in chariots. But Alexander's forces lined up in their usual formation, and Alexander raced his cavalry toward the Persians, outflanking them. In the middle of his line with his infantry, Darius moved over to block Alexander, but Alexander's horses charged right through Darius's infantry. Darius's chariots came rumbling out, but Alexander's Bulgarian javelin-throwers massacred the men and horses.

Horrified, Darius broke and ran. Before Alexander could chase him down, he received word that the Indian and Scythian cavalries had trapped General Parmenion's left flank. Alexander raced to his aid in a lethal conflict that killed sixty elite Macedonian cavalrymen. Finally, the Persian army heard Darius had left the battle and likewise fled. Alexander marched into Babylon with no resistance, and the people announced him as the new ruler of Persia.

Darius fled with a small remnant of his army to Media, but his Bactrian satrap Bessus murdered him; Bessus then proclaimed himself king. After ordering his rival's royal burial, Alexander began organizing his empire. He appointed leaders to his provinces, keeping all the Persian satraps who swore loyalty to him. His next task was to hunt Bessus down in the east and execute him for assassinating King Darius. But the Bactrian chieftains betrayed Bessus; Alexander found him chained to a stake and ordered him sent to Persia for trial and execution.

Alexander's soldiers were weary and ready to go home to their wives and children. But Alexander wanted to keep going to the empire's eastern borders, to the Ganges River, the "end of the world." Alexander reached the Jaxartes River, the empire's eastern boundary. Then, the Scythians attacked, and an arrow pierced Alexander's shin, breaking his calf bone.

Nevertheless, Alexander pummeled the nomadic Scythians but could not thwart the Bactrian and Sogdian guerilla attacks. A rock struck his head in the 329 BCE Siege of Cyropolis (in present-day Tajikistan). The violent head injury (on top of multiple previous head injuries) caused transient blindness and a temporary inability to speak or walk.

Alexander's troops were increasingly edgy and demoralized; they just wanted to go home, but Alexander wanted to press farther east. Alexander annoyed his troops further by wearing Persian clothing and expecting everyone to prostrate themselves before him in the Persian fashion. His erratic behavior turned lethal when he got drunk and murdered Cleitus the Black, his close friend who had once saved his life.

While fighting the Sogdians in 327 BCE, Alexander captured Roxana, the lovely daughter of the Bactrian Lord Oxyartes. Oxyartes surrendered immediately to save his daughter and other family members, but Alexander was captivated by his captive! Alexander married her, overriding the objections of his appalled generals. He appointed Oxyartes as the satrap of the Hindu Kush mountain region. Hopefully, his father-in-law would rein in the rest of the Bactrians and Sogdians.

Alexander forged on, scaling the lofty, snow-encrusted Hindu Kush mountains at the 3,500-foot Khyber Pass between Afghanistan and Pakistan. During his descent into the Indian subcontinent, he fought the vicious Assaceni and Aspasii tribes. On the swollen banks of the Jhelum River, he faced the Pauravas' king Porus. It was monsoon season, and crossing the churning river was impossible. Alexander camped across the river from Porus, keeping most of his troops out of sight. By doing this, he was able to trick Porus into thinking his army was smaller.

During the nights, his cavalry searched for a place to cross the river and found one seventeen miles upstream. While General Craterus and part of the Greek forces created a distraction across the river from Porus, Alexander and the rest of the men crept upstream, out of sight. His forces crossed the river in small boats or held onto inflated skins. Then they moved downstream toward Porus's forces, who moved into ranks to face Alexander.

Alexander positioned his cavalry on both flanks using a pincer maneuver in what is now known as the Battle of the Hydaspes. A wall of bristling eighteen-foot-sarissas broke the Indian war elephants' charge. The elephants killed many of Alexander's men, but the long pikes panicked the beasts into turning around and charging back, crushing as many of Porus's men as they had Alexander's. Alexander then implemented a hammer and anvil maneuver: one force encircling the enemy while the other attacked frontally, bringing a stunning victory that won control of Punjab.

Alexander's quest to reach the "edge of the world," the great river of India, dissipated when his soldiers mutinied. After years of fighting in the Persian Empire, the men were battle-weary, and they heard India was assembling giant armies. A peeved Alexander led the men down the Indus River to the coast. He sent half his army by the Arabian Sea and the Persian Gulf to Persia. Alexander marched back with the rest of his men over the harsh Makran desert, where the extreme heat and thirst killed one-third of his army. After arriving in Persia, Alexander paid off the debts of his remaining soldiers.

And then Alexander threw a massive, multi-couple wedding. At a lavish feast, he married eighty Persian princesses to his Macedonian nobility, intermingling the leading families to cement the takeover of the empire. Alexander married two princesses: King Darius's daughter Stateira, who had been his captive for a decade, and Parysatis II, daughter of King Artaxerxes III. Alexander was thrilled to learn his beloved wife Roxana had conceived, but he would never hold his son in his arms.

Alexander fell ill with a fever in 323 BCE and died within two weeks. The indomitable warrior who had never lost a battle and created a new empire stretching from Greece to the Indus Valley lost his final struggle at only thirty-two. Alexander's fellow Macedonians carried his body in a honey-filled sarcophagus back to Macedon for burial. But on their journey, Alexander's general,

Ptolemy (Egypt's new pharaoh), stole the coffin! It remained a prized possession in Alexandria for centuries; Roman emperors even made pilgrimages to view the sarcophagus. Historians are not quite sure where his tomb is today, but there are several theories. Perhaps one day, it will be unearthed.

What happened to Persia? Alexander's unexpected death created chaos in the empire. Roxana, who gave birth to their son after his death, killed his Persian wives. One of Alexander's generals, Cassander, later poisoned Roxana and her son. Alexander's generals contended over the vast territory that spanned three continents. They finally divided the empire into three: Macedon to the Antigonus dynasty, Egypt to the Ptolemy dynasty, and the remnants of the Persian Empire to the Seleucus dynasty.

The new Seleucid Empire, founded by Alexander's general Seleucus I Nicator, lasted from 312 to 63 BCE as a center of Hellenistic culture. At its zenith, the Persian-Seleucid Empire stretched from Anatolia (Turkey) down through the Levant on the Mediterranean and west through Mesopotamia and Iran to today's Kuwait, Afghanistan, and Turkmenistan. As other kingdoms rose to power over the centuries, the Persian-Seleucid Empire gradually declined until it was reduced to an area encompassing Syria. General Pompey of Rome ultimately overthrew the remnants of the empire in 63 BCE.

Conclusion

Ancient Mesopotamia's legacy was truly revolutionary. The "cradle of civilization" fostered innovations that transformed the world through its many inventions, law codes, and political organizations that integrated numerous cultures under one central government. The story of civilization—the inception of the wheel, the concept of time, writing, schools, measurements, basic counting, higher math, and hydraulic engineering—all began in ancient Mesopotamia.

Development and innovation thrived in this semi-arid land that was fed by two great rivers flowing from the Taurus Mountains into the Persian Gulf. Farming settlements blossomed into the world's first urban centers, where people built sophisticated buildings and infrastructure like roads, sewer drains, defensive walls, and irrigation. They gazed at the sky and mapped it, dividing the year into twelve months named after the constellations. They observed the retrograde motion of the planets, predicted helical rising, and knew when lunar and solar eclipses would happen.

Childlike pictures scratched into wet clay morphed into the complex cuneiform script used to record over a dozen spoken languages. The Mesopotamians used cuneiform to write the first epic poems, the first hymns, the first histories, and the first law codes. They developed the wheel to speed the task of pottery-making, then realized it could be utilized for transportation. Simple carts hauling bricks or farm produce evolved into chariots that could race along at thirty-five miles per hour.

For over a millennium, the incipient city-states were independent and self-contained. Gradually, one city would rise to "kingship" over the others, becoming the regional center of power, trade, and religion. These eventually developed into multi-ethnic empires covering hundreds of miles, then thousands, and then multiple continents. They developed highways and postal systems to travel and communicate over massive distances.

Mesopotamia's inventions and firsts continue to be relevant, and we still use many of them in some form today. Think of all the ways we use the wheel today! Trains, planes, trucks, cars, motorcycles, and bicycles: almost all our transportation modes use the wheel, which was invented in ancient Sumer. Even boats and ships use them with the ship's wheel, rudder, and pulley systems. Let's not forget other modern ways we use the wheel like the cogwheel, the propeller, the gyroscope, and the turbine.

Mesopotamia instituted the first schools to teach students to read and write the first written language. Try to imagine a world without schools today. Everyone needs basic literacy and math to function at the lowest level, but we live in a constantly changing world. Education, in some form, enables us to keep up with all the recent technologies. Our schooling helps us understand the world around us, like what's going on with disease control, government, and economics.

How many times throughout the day does the ordinary person use basic counting, math, and even higher math? We give little thought to measuring ingredients or doubling recipes. We calculate how much weight we've gained or lost when we step on the scale. We use basic math to pay bills, balance the checkbook, and make a budget. When we do home renovation projects, we calculate how much tile, carpet, or fabric to buy, which requires basic geometry.

The simple math that all of us use every day was developed over four thousand years ago in Mesopotamia.

How did ancient Mesopotamia's innovations and explosions of knowledge in various fields pave the way for modern technologies that have molded society as we know it today? For one thing, the ancient Mesopotamians didn't stop with developing basic counting and measurements. They progressed with higher mathematical sciences that contribute to the technology base underlying a multitude of functions in our world.

The ancient Mesopotamians' higher mathematics are implemented in manufacturing new or improved products and in weather forecasts that use computer simulations and mathematical modeling. Geometry contributes to fuel economy by designing advanced wing foils on aircraft. Math is applied to technological topics such as structural mechanics, optics, building construction, and engineering thermodynamics.

Mathematics forms the groundwork for computer technology that implements abstract language, logical deductions, and algorithms. Healthcare technology and research use math to draw up statistical graphs of pandemic infections, hospitalizations, and deaths or track vaccine rates and efficacy. Medical laboratories use math in converting grams to micrograms and mass to molar conversions. Higher math is used in the statistical analysis of standard deviations and standard curves.

The ancient Mesopotamians also developed technology in irrigation systems and hydraulic engineering. They created levees and dams to channel river water and later invented the qanat irrigation system to pull water up from underground aquifers. Even the oldest Sumerian cities had sewer drains for their houses. The basic hydraulic engineering innovated by ancient Mesopotamians has continued to develop, and its applications in the modern world are widespread. We still have dams, levees, and water distribution networks, but we also have automated sprinkler systems, sewage collection, and stormwater management. Fluid dynamic principles are utilized in aeronautical, mechanical, and even traffic engineering.

The ancient Mesopotamian law codes and their political and organizational practices are still relevant and applied in some form today. We all need concepts of basic morality, an understanding of right and wrong, that lifts us out of chaos and into true civilization. When Ur-Nammu and Hammurabi wrote their law codes, they first had to consider the underlying morality, and they had to decide what was good for society and what was disruptive. Their law codes sought to protect all citizens, especially the weak and disenfranchised, from harmful behaviors by others. Our legislative branches today still struggle with writing laws that stop detrimental behaviors and protect the safety and rights of all citizens.

The writers of ancient law codes and the political leaders of ancient Mesopotamia also had to contemplate the concepts of fairness to all, regardless of social standing. They had to consider how to stop immorality and crime in society. They had to ponder justice so that the strong didn't prevail over the weak or the wicked over the innocent. Cyrus the Great *was* great because he seemed to genuinely champion protection and opportunities for all, regardless of ethnicity, religion, or ideology. Today's legislative and judicial branches worldwide still struggle to ensure that fairness extends to everyone and that justice prevails against corruptness and exploitation.

Although the once-spectacular cities have sunk into the desert sands, the ideas of the ancient Mesopotamians continue to persevere and evolve in virtually all knowledge we have regarding astronomy, math, literacy, law, transportation, communication, engineering, architecture, and government. Although the once-magnificent ancient civilizations have faded into the mist of history, the ideals of the ancient Mesopotamians continue to guide us today: our understanding of the spiritual world, our appreciation of art and beauty, and our concepts of morality, tenacity, truth, justice, fairness, and friendship. Ancient Mesopotamia lives on through us all.

Here's another book by Enthralling History that you might like

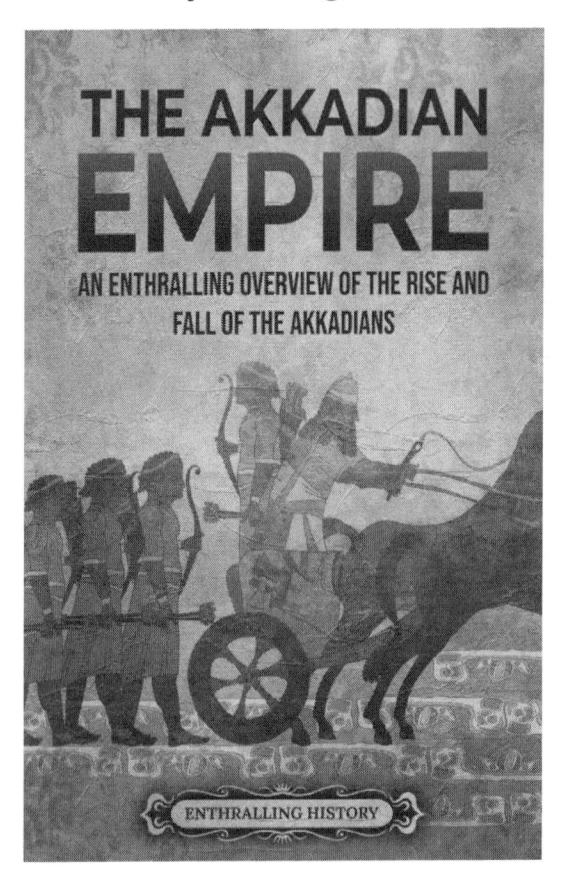

THE AKKADIAN EMPIRE
AN ENTHRALLING OVERVIEW OF THE RISE AND FALL OF THE AKKADIANS

ENTHRALLING HISTORY

Free limited time bonus

Stop for a moment. We have a free bonus set up for you. The problem is this: we forget 90% of everything that we read after 7 days. Crazy fact, right? Here's the solution: we've created a printable, 1-page pdf summary for this book that you're reading now. All you have to do to get your free pdf summary is to go to the following website: **https://livetolearn.lpages.co/enthrallinghistory/**

Once you do, it will be intuitive. Enjoy, and thank you!

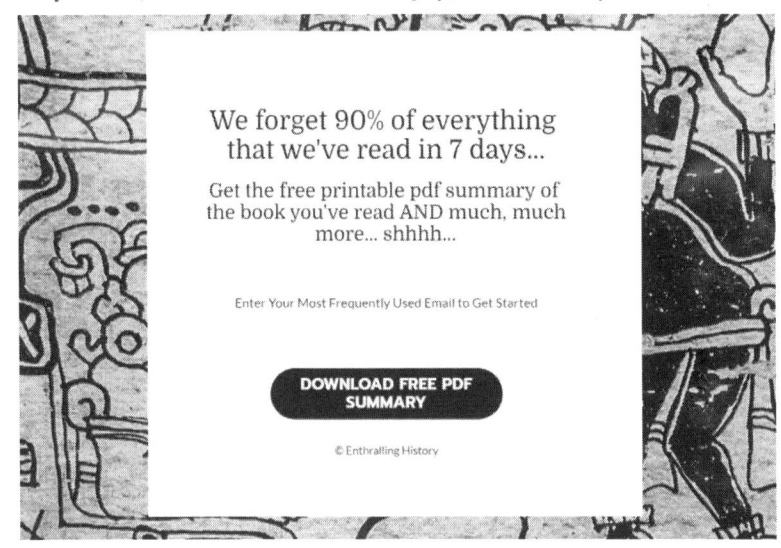

Bibliography

Bertman, Stephen. *Handbook to Life in Ancient Mesopotamia.* Oxford: Oxford University Press, 2005.

Clark, Peter. *Zoroastrianism: An Introduction to an Ancient Faith (Beliefs & Practices).* East Sussex: Sussex Academic Press, 1998.

Dalley, Stephanie. *Myths from Mesopotamia Creation, the Flood, Gilgamesh, and Others.* Oxford: Oxford University Press, 2008.

Dalley, Stephanie. "Old Babylonian Tablets from Nineveh; And Possible Pieces of Early Gilgamesh Epic." In *Iraq* 63 (2001): 155-67. https://doi.org/10.2307/4200507

Editors. "The World's Oldest Writing." In *Archaeology,* May/June 2016. https://www.archaeology.org/issues/213-features/4326-cuneiform-the-world-s-oldest-writing

Enuma Elish: The Seven Tablets of Creation. Translated by Leonard William King. Sacred

Texts.com. Accessed November 20, 2021.

https://www.sacred-texts.com/ane/stc/index.htm

Eppihimer, Melissa. "Assembling King and State: The Statues of Manishtushu and the Consolidation of Akkadian Kingship." In

American Journal of Archaeology 114, no. 3 (2010): 365-80. http://www.jstor.org/stable/25684286

Frymer-Kensky, Tikva. "The Tribulations of Marduk: The So-Called 'Marduk Ordeal Text.'" *Journal of the American Oriental Society* 103, no. 1 (1983): 131-41. https://doi.org/10.2307/601866

Hritz, Carrie, Jennifer Pournelle, Jennifer Smith, and سميث جنيفر. *Revisiting the Sealands: Report of Preliminary Ground Reconnaissance in the Hammar District, Dhi Qar and Basra Governorates, Iraq.* Iraq 74 (2012): 37-49. http://www.jstor.org/stable/23349778

Jacobsen, Thorkild. "The Assumed Conflict between Sumerians and Semites in Early Mesopotamian History." In *Journal of the American Oriental Society* 59, no. 4 (1939): 485-95. https://doi.org/10.2307/594482

Kramer, Samuel Noah. *The Sumerians: Their History, Culture, and Character.* Chicago: University of Chicago Press, 1971.

Marriage of Martu. Translated by J. A. Black, G. Cunningham, E. Robson, and G. Zólyomi. The Electronic Text Corpus of Sumerian Literature, Oxford 1998. Accessed November 17, 2021. https://www.gatewaystobabylon.com/myths/texts/classic/martu.htm

Mesopotamia: A Captivating Guide to Ancient Mesopotamian History and Civilizations, Hammurabi, and the Persian Empire. Captivating History, 2019.

Moorey, P. R. S. "The 'Plano-Convex Building' at Kish and Early Mesopotamian Palaces." *Iraq* 26, no. 2 (1964): 83-98. https://doi.org/10.2307/4199767

Oppenheim, Leo. *Ancient Mesopotamia: Portrait of a Dead Civilization.* Chicago: University of Chicago Press, 1977.

Petrovich, Douglas. "Identifying Nimrod of Genesis 10 with Sargon of Akkad by Exegetical and Archaeological Means." In *Journal of the Evangelical Theological Society* 56, no. 2 (2013): 273-305.

https://www.etsjets.org/files/JETS-PDFs/56/56-2/JETS_56-2_273-305_Petrovich.pdf

Pollock, Susan. *Ancient Mesopotamia*. Cambridge: Cambridge University Press, 1999.

Ponchia, Simonetta, Saana Svärd, and Kazuko Watanabe. "Slaves, Serfs, and Prisoners in Imperial Assyria (IX–VII Cent. BC). A Review of Written Sources." In *State Archives of Assyria Bulletin* 23 (2017): 157-179. https://www.academia.edu/36199877/Slaves_Serfs_and_Prisoners_in_Imperial_Assyria_IX_VII_Cent_BC_A_Review_of_written_sources?auto=download

Postgate, Nicholas. *Early Mesopotamia: Society and Economy at the Dawn of History*. Oxfordshire: Routledge, 1994.

Sackrider, Scott. "The History of Astronomy in Ancient Mesopotamia." In *The NEKAAL Observer* 234. https://nekaal.org/observer/ar/ObserverArticle234.pdf

Speiser, E. A. "Some Factors in the Collapse of Akkad." In *Journal of the American Oriental Society* 72, no. 3 (1952): 97–101. https://doi.org/10.2307/594938

Sumerian King List. Translated by Jean-Vincent Scheil, Stephen Langdon, and Thorkild Jacobsen. Livius, accessed October 20, 2021. https://www.livius.org/sources/content/anet/266-the-sumerian-king-list/#Translation

Teall, Emily K. (2014) "Medicine and Doctoring in Ancient Mesopotamia." In *Grand Valley Journal of History* 3:1, Article 2. https://scholarworks.gvsu.edu/gvjh/vol3/iss1/2

The *Assyrian King List*. Translated by Jean-Jacques Glassner. Livius, accessed November 12, 2021. https://www.livius.org/sources/content/anet/564-566-the-assyrian-king-list

"The Code of Hammurabi." Translated by L.W. King. In *The Avalon Project: Documents in Law, History, and Diplomacy.* Yale Law School: Lillian Goldman Law Library. Accessed November 27, 2001. https://avalon.law.yale.edu/ancient/hamframe.asp

The *Epic of Atrahasis.* Translated by B. R. Foster. Livius, accessed October 18, 2021. https://www.livius.org/sources/content/anet/104-106-the-epic-of-atrahasis

The *Epic of Gilgamesh.* Translated by N. K. Sandars. London: Penguin Classics, 1960.

The Tanakh: Full Text. Jewish Virtual Library: A Project of AICE. 1997. https://www.jewishvirtuallibrary.org/the-tanakh-full-text

Van De Mieroop, Marc. *A History of the Ancient Near East ca. 3000 - 323 BC.* Hoboken: Blackwell Publishing, 2006.

Van De Mieroop, Marc. *King Hammurabi of Babylon: A Biography.* Hoboken: Blackwell Publishing, 2004.

Vargyas, Péter. "Sennacherib's Alleged Half-Shekel Coins." In *Journal of Near Eastern Studies,* 61, no. 2 (2002): 111-15. http://www.jstor.org/stable/545291